# Forensic Anthropology Laboratory Manual

This manual provides students in academic laboratory courses with hands-on experience of the major processes of forensic anthropology. Designed to accompany the textbook *Introduction to Forensic Anthropology*, the manual introduces core procedures and protocol, with exercise worksheets to reinforce the methodologies of forensic anthropology and enhance student comprehension. For the fourth edition, the manual has been updated in line with the textbook, incorporating new methods, figures, and worksheets. Each chapter contains explanations of the terminology, osteological features, and measurements needed to understand each of the topics. Chapters may be covered in one session or multiple sessions and include lists of both basic and optional lab materials, enabling instructors to tailor each lab to the resources they have available.

**Steven N. Byers** has a Ph.D. in Anthropology from the University of New Mexico (UNM), USA. Now retired, he worked for a number of years on various campuses of UNM, teaching courses in Forensic Anthropology, Biological Anthropology, and Archaeology. He is currently serving on the Anthropology Consensus Body of the American Academy of Forensic Sciences Standards Board, in addition to focusing on Southeastern United States bioarchaeology. Byers' publications with Routledge also include this title's sister volume, *Introduction to Forensic Anthropology* (in its 5th edition).

D1710169

Praise for this edition:

"The fourth edition of *Forensic Anthropology Laboratory Manual* is a welcome and necessary complement to the textbook, *Introduction to Forensic Anthropology*. Designed to work in conjunction with the book chapters, the lab manual elaborates on specific concepts and provides an easy to follow lab exercise that illustrates the application of those concepts. Topics that were once difficult to convey to students have now been simplified and explained in this lab manual, allowing the student to fully immerse in the current and challenging field of Forensic Anthropology."

Ann Marie Mires, *Director of Forensic Criminology at Anna Maria College, USA*

"Steven Byers' fourth edition is the new gold standard for forensic methods. Students use the lab manual to understand and easily master the hands-on techniques of forensics. Each exercise clearly links lecture content to experiential learning. This edition isn't just required reading for the students, it's also my favorite lab partner."

Monica Faraldo, *Department of Anthropology, University of Miami, USA*

# Forensic Anthropology Laboratory Manual

**FOURTH EDITION**

To be used in conjunction with
*Introduction to Forensic Anthropology* Fifth Edition

## Steven N. Byers

LONDON AND NEW YORK

Fourth edition published 2017
by Routledge
2 Park Square, Milton Park, Abingdon, Oxon OX14 4RN

and by Routledge
711 Third Avenue, New York, NY 10017

*Routledge is an imprint of the Taylor & Francis Group, an informa business*

© 2017 Steven N. Byers

First edition published by Pearson 2005

*British Library Cataloguing-in-Publication Data*
A catalogue record for this book is available from the British Library

*Library of Congress Cataloging-in-Publication Data*
Names: Byers, Steven N.
Title: Forensic anthropology laboratory manual / Steven N. Byers.
Description: Fourth edition. | Milton Park, Abingdon, Oxon ;
    New York, NY : Routledge, 2016.
Identifiers: LCCN 2016006771 | ISBN 9781138690738
    (pbk. : alk. paper) | ISBN 9781315535371 (ebook)
Subjects: LCSH: Forensic anthropology.
Classification: LCC GN69.8 .B93 2016 | DDC 614/.17—dc23
LC record available at http://lccn.loc.gov/2016006771

ISBN: 978-1-138-69073-8 (pbk)
ISBN: 978-1-315-53537-1 (ebk)


Typeset in Sabon
by Apex CoVantage, LLC

To those of you who find forensic anthropology as fascinating as I do

# Contents

# Preface

This laboratory manual formalizes a college-level introductory laboratory course in forensic anthropology. Because of the growing interest in "things forensic" (as evidenced by the number of courses offered nationwide), a manual that presents students with "hands-on" experience in the methods of forensic anthropology seems in order. Also, my editor encountered many instructors who asked if such a manual could be written because their students desired to apply the methods learned in lecture classes. Due to the level of interest expressed through these various venues, this project was undertaken.

To reduce redundancy as much as possible, this manual is designed to be used in conjunction with the book *Introduction to Forensic Anthropology*, Fifth Edition (referred to in this manual simply as "the textbook"). There is a one-to-one correspondence between the chapters of these two publications; each chapter in this manual refers to narrative and figures in the textbook. Also, this lab manual uses many of the drawings from the textbook (with additions where it was considered desirable) to avoid constant shuffling between the two. However, because none of the photos from the textbook are included, it is paramount that students use the textbook when performing these labs so that they maximize their exposure to the visual information needed to understand the concepts presented.

Each chapter in this manual has a similar outline. After an opening paragraph describing the purpose of the lab, **Learning Objectives** are presented followed by **Expected Outcomes**. Next comes a list of **Minimum Materials**, which is an inventory of those supplies that the author believes are absolutely necessary to do that particular lab task (if these materials are not available, the lab should not be attempted). This section is followed by a list of **Optional Materials**, which includes extra (usually hard-to-find) resources that are not necessary for the lab to be completed but, if present, lend richness to the exercises. These sections are followed by instructions for performing the individual **Exercises** in the lab. Most chapters contain several of these, numbered for convenience, which can be included or omitted depending on the presence of materials. Following the exercises is a **Note to Instructors**, which contains hints that help instructors offer the exercises to their students. Finally, at the end of each lab are **Exercise Worksheets** that are designed to be completed by students, removed from this manual, and turned in to instructors for grading. In some labs, there are several copies of the same worksheet so that students can perform the exercises on several different lab specimens. In all, it is hoped that this organization will help both students and instructors in the laboratory process.

As with any publication of this nature, many people contributed to its completion. The author thanks the following reviewers who evaluated the prospectus for this work and recommended its publication: A. Midori Albert, University of North Carolina–Wilmington; Kelly Ann Costa, Franklin Pierce College; and Debra L. Martin, Hampshire College. I also thank my editor Katherine Ong and her editorial assistants, Elizabeth Thomasson and Lola Harre, for their support and tolerance during the revision of this manual. Finally, I thank Taylor & Francis for allowing me the opportunity to present this publication to you.

# Note to Instructors

The following notes are intended to help instructors offer the labs given in this manual. They are based on the author's own experiences and are offered in the spirit of preventing you from "re-inventing the wheel":

1. As stated in the Preface, the textbook is needed by students to complete the lab assignments.
2. If you do not have enough materials for your lab, you can divide students into teams of three to five persons. This is not unwieldy and usually generates lively discussions and friendly competitions. Even if you have plenty of materials, division into teams is a valuable adjunct to the laboratory process. Forensic anthropology stresses the team approach, so early exposure to teamwork in these labs is useful even at the introductory level.
3. Sometimes, real human skeletal remains may not be available, or those that are may not show the necessary characteristics being taught in a lab (e.g., bullet wounds, accessory ossicles). In these cases, casts can be obtained from a number of different sources that illustrate some of these conditions. Although those with the level of detail of real bone are available (at a high cost), even the low-cost plastic casts can be used with good effect in a lab of this type. See the following Sources of Materials section for more information.
4. When materials are not available for a specific lab, simply skip that chapter and spend more time on those where you do have materials. For example, if you do not have any skeletal remains exhibiting water or fire damage, you may want to skip Chapter 16, "Postmortem Changes to Bone," and concentrate on chapters such as Chapter 8, "Attribution of Sex," where you can spend one week on the pelvis and one on the skull and other bones.
5. As stated in the Preface, this manual has the same number of chapters as the textbook; indeed, they even have the same name. This will allow you to offer labs that follow the topics you present in class. However, at times, this may be unwieldy. For example, anthropometric and osteometric instruments are presented in Chapter 1 of both the textbook and this manual. However, these implements are not used again until Chapter 7, "Attribution of Ancestry." This hiatus between their introduction and eventual use may make it desirable to start the lab with Chapter 2, "Basics of Human Osteology and Odontology," so that two (or more) weeks can be spent on this all-important topic. Then, the exercises of Chapter 1 can be completed when the instruments are first used.

## Sources of Materials

Although real human skeletons are best for forensic anthropology, usually the availability of bones displaying some of the features discussed in this lab is severely limited. In these cases, casts may have to be obtained that exhibit conditions such as gunshot wounds, blunt trauma, nonmetric variations, as well as variations within the basic demographic groups. The following is a list of sources that the author either knows of, or has used in the past.

*Carolina Biological Supply:* This company markets real human skeletons as well as low-cost casts (see its website at www.carolina.com). Its casts are made of a durable plastic that will withstand handling over many years without undue wear and tear. This company also offers specimens from Bone Clones, Inc. (see below).

*A. Daigger & Company, Inc.:* This company markets plastic human skeletons (see its website at www.daigger.com); I do not have experience with its materials.

*Bone Clones, Inc.:* This company provides highly durable resin casts that afford good detail (see its website at www.boneclones.com). As of this writing, it provides human skulls from various ancestral groups, sets of bones comparing males and females (e.g., skull, pelvis, femur), skulls and skeletons of adults and subadults, and immature individual bones (e.g., femur with epiphyses, individual bones of the os coxa). It also markets a fairly large collection of forensic and pathological specimens. In addition to this collection, it has a wide variety of casts of nonhuman animal bone.

*France Casting:* This company provides detailed, durable casts of various human and nonhuman bones (see Dr. France's website at www.francecasts.com). The list of casts offered by this company is similar to that of Bone Clones; that is, skulls of different ancestral groups, male versus female pelvises, trephined skull, nonhuman animals, and so on. In addition, this company provides a good assortment of bones with pathological conditions as well as casts of pubic faces showing changes with age.

*The BoneRoom:* This company bills itself as "the web's premier natural history store" and offers an impressive number of bones and casts of both human and nonhuman remains. Although I have not seen any of their material, the website photos indicate good quality. You can access their store from their website at www.boneroom.com.

*American 3B Scientific:* This company offers a large assortment of supplies, charts, and software related to scientific activities and health care. They offer human skeleton casts that are reasonably priced, but the level of detail is unknown. Please see their website at www.a3bs.com.

*Skullduggery:* This company sells a limited number of human skull casts: one male, one female, a skull with trephination, and one with cranial deformation. I have no direct experience with their products, but the photos on their website (www.skullduggery.com) indicate good detail.

## Instruments

The various calipers used by professional forensic and other biological anthropologists can be obtained from several sources: Paleotech Concepts (see its website at www.paleo-tech.com) and Siber, Hegner and Co. (see the www.dksh.ch website; search for "GPM Anthropological Instruments"). However, because of their expense, most of these calipers can use a considerable amount of a laboratory budget and may be out of reach of many institutions. Fortunately, less-expensive alternatives are available. Cheap equivalents of the spreading caliper can be obtained from stores that specialize in tools (I purchased several sets for less than $4 each). Carolina Biological Supply has plastic versions called "bow calipers." Additionally, calipers can be constructed from heavy cardboard, thin wood, or masonite. These do not have scales such as those illustrated in Figure 1.5 of the textbook, However, the length of a measurement can be obtained by placing the separated tips against a millimeter rule available from any office supply store.

Inexpensive alternatives to the sliding calipers illustrated in Figure 1.5 of the textbook are available from many types of stores, especially those specializing in tools. Some have only a 4-inch (100-millimeter) spread, while others go to 6 inches (150 millimeters). (I purchased several plastic sets that had a 6-inch spread for only $1 each.) These even allow for measurements of distances less than a millimeter, although this feature would not be used often in a class of this nature. Finally, an osteometric (bone) board can be constructed from 1" × 6" lumber as illustrated in Figures 1.5 and 1.6 in the textbook.

# Note to Students

The author thanks you for your interest in forensic anthropology; it is because of you that I wrote this manual. The following notes are offered in the spirit of making your lab experience more enjoyable and fruitful.

1. *Introduction to Forensic Anthropology*, Fifth Edition (referred to in this manual simply as "the textbook") is a necessary part of your labs. This manual was not written to be a stand-alone publication; rather, it refers constantly to the chapters in the textbook. Thus, you will need to bring both the textbook and this manual to your lab when completing the exercises.
2. Although some of the labs presented herein may seem simple, they are similar to (and in some cases, exactly like) the methods used by forensic anthropologists. Thus, by doing the work presented in this manual, you will gain valuable insight into the everyday workings of forensic anthropology.
3. The exercises presented in this lab manual will not make you an expert in forensic anthropology. Although there is a natural tendency to feel that you have gained considerable knowledge after devoting an entire quarter or semester to a lab of this nature, you must resist this temptation. Forensic anthropology is like any other subject; it requires a significant amount of time and experience to become proficient. I have viewed hundreds of human skeletons during my career, yet still encounter conditions I have never seen before. Recognize the limits of what you learn in these labs, and what there remains to learn.

# 1 Introduction

As described in the textbook, forensic anthropologists employ two main methods for gathering data: anthroposcopy and osteometry. In later chapters, you will learn the basics of anthroposcopy; however, in this chapter, you will be introduced to the various ways that bones are measured. This involves using anthropometric instruments, such as calipers or an osteometric (bone) board, to obtain dimensions of osteological structures, such as the skull, pelvis, or single bones. (Interestingly, many of these measurements are quantifications of the anthroposcopic characteristics that aid in the identification of demographic aspects of the skeleton.) These implements regularly employ the metric system, while much of the medicolegal community uses U.S. customary units (i.e., inches, feet, ounces, pounds). Thus, part of this lab involves converting from metric to U.S. measure.

## Learning Objectives

The purpose of this lab is to acquaint you with the instruments used by forensic anthropologists in their work. These include spreading calipers, sliding calipers, and the osteometric (also called bone) board (see Figure 1.5 in the textbook). In addition, you will learn (or review, depending on your exposure) the metric system that is used in this type of work.

## Expected Outcomes

By the end of this lab, you should be able to:

- Recognize the three basic instruments of the forensic anthropologist: spreading caliper, sliding caliper, and bone board.
- Take measurements of bones using these instruments.
- Properly read the scales on these instruments.
- Convert metric measurements into U.S. measure.

## Minimum Materials

Sliding caliper (with scale), 4-inch or 6-inch
Spreading caliper (without scale)
Osteometric (bone) board
Any long limb bones, human or nonhuman, plastic or real
Human humerus, plastic or real
Human skull, plastic or real

## Optional Materials

Spreading caliper (with scale)

## Exercise 1.1: Basic Instruments and Their Use

Before commencing this exercise, read the section Data Gathering Methods in Chapter 1 of the textbook. Now, take one of the instruments (sliding caliper, spreading caliper, or bone board) and determine how it operates (see Figure 1.5 in the textbook). For the sliding caliper and bone board, there is a slide that moves on the long axis of the instrument; this instrument has a fixed end. For the spreading caliper, the tips can be separated from each other by swinging the arms on the hinge joint that connects them. Whichever instrument you are examining, move the tips until they contact each other. If there is a scale, determine the point where "0" is read; this is the point from which you will read the distances measured by the instrument. If there is no scale, a millimeter ruler will need to be used to determine the distance between the tips of the instrument.

Try to measure the length of one of the bones provided by the lab instructor. If a long limb bone will fit within its jaws, use a sliding caliper (see Figure 1.8 of the textbook); if not, then the bone board should be used (see Figure 1.6 of the textbook). If measuring a bone, skull, or other structure that prevents a sliding caliper from contacting the two points being measured, use the spreading caliper. Now, enter the bone/structure name and the measurements in either millimeters or centimeters on the lines on Exercise Worksheet 1.1, provided at the end of this lab. Measure at least one bone with each of the instruments to become familiar with their use; enter your results in the worksheet.

## Exercise 1.2: Metric System and U.S. Measure

The following is a brief overview of the metric system and its relationship to U.S. measure. The metric system, as used in forensic anthropology, involves both measurements of length and weight. Length is measured in terms of millimeters (mm), centimeters (cm), and meters (m), while weights are given in grams (gm) and kilograms (kg). Table 1.1 presents both the relationship of these units to one another, as well as the conversion factor to U.S. measure.

There is one situation in forensic anthropology in which you will be required to convert from metric to U.S. lengths. This is during stature reconstruction, where the formulae for calculating this statistic from long limb bones gives height in the metric system, while law enforcement personnel expects this amount in U.S. measure. This conversion is easily accomplished if you own a calculator with a metric/U.S. conversion button. If not, you can use the following steps to make this change:

**Step 1.** Divide the metric measurement (in centimeters) by 2.54; this is the number of centimeters in an inch and will yield the height in inches.

**Step 2.** Divide the result of step 1 by 12, ignoring any digits to the right of the decimal point. This is the number of feet in the stature estimation.

**Step 3.** Multiply the result in step 2 by 12 and subtract it from the result of step 1. The remainder is the number of inches in the stature estimation.

**Step 4.** The number of feet is the result of step 2, while the number of inches is the result of step 3.

*Table 1.1* Unit Conversions

| Metric | | | | |
|---|---|---|---|---|
| 1 millimeter (mm) | = | 1/10 cm | = | 1/1000 m |
| 1 centimeter (cm) | = | 10 mm | = | 1/100 m |
| 1 meter (m) | = | 1000 mm | = | 100 cm |
| 1 gram (gm) | = | 1/1000 kg | | |
| 1 kilogram (kg) | = | 1000 gm | | |
| **U.S. Measure Equivalents** | | | | |
| 1 inch (1") | = | 25.4 mm | = | 2.54 cm |
| 1 foot (1') | = | 305 mm | = | 30.5 cm |
| 1 pound (lb) | = | 453 gm | = | 0.453 kg |

Next, measure a humerus provided by the lab instructor, and calculate the living stature of the person represented by this bone on Exercise Worksheet 1.1 by multiplying its length by 5 (as mentioned in the textbook, this results in a rough estimate of living height). Now, convert this amount into feet and inches using either the calculator button or the steps outlined earlier and reproduced on Exercise Worksheet 1.2. Do this for several bones until you feel comfortable measuring the length of this bone, calculating stature, and converting the stature from the metric system to U.S. measure.

## NOTE TO INSTRUCTORS

As stated earlier, the instruments used by professional forensic and other biological anthropologists can be quite expensive and hard to find, but do not be discouraged. Perfectly acceptable (albeit, not optimal) substitutes can be found from various stores specializing in tools or from Carolina Biological Supply. I have found that students respond well to labs that use even the most crude of spreading and sliding calipers; they find the subject matter so interesting that the lack of sophistication does not disturb them.

**Exercise Worksheet 1.1: Basic Instruments and Their Use**

Name: _____   Date:_____

Case/Accession number:_____

Sliding caliper:

Bone/Structure: _____

Measurement: _____

Spreading caliper: _____

Bone/Structure: _____

Measurement: _____

Osteometric (bone) board: _____

Bone/Structure: _____

Measurement: _____

Humerus 1 length: _____ × 5 = _____
(stature)

Humerus 2 length: _____ × 5 = _____
(stature)

Humerus 3 length: _____ × 5 = _____
(stature)

**Exercise Worksheet 1.2: Metric System and U.S. Measure**

Name: _____  Date: _____

Case/Accession number: _____

# Humerus 1

1. _____  _____ ÷ 2.54 = _____
   (stature in centimeters)                          (stature in inches)

2. _____ ÷ 12 = _____
   (stature in inches)                               (stature in feet, ignore digits to right of decimal)

3. _____ − (_____ × 12) = _____
   (stature in inches)        (stature in feet)              (reminder)

4. Stature: _____’ and = _____”
   (stature in feet)                                (reminder)

# Humerus 2

1. _____ ÷ 2.54 = _____
   (stature in centimeters)                          (stature in inches)

2. _____ ÷ 12 = _____
   (stature in inches)                               (stature in feet, ignore digits to right of decimal)

3. _____ − (_____ × 12) = _____
   (stature in inches)        (stature in feet)              (reminder)

4. Stature: _____’ and = _____”
   (stature in feet)                            (reminder)

# 2   Basics of Human Osteology and Odontology

Chapter 2 in the textbook provides an overview of the skeletal and dental structures of the human body. To facilitate your understanding of the skeleton, the standard anatomical position is described along with a list of terms of anatomical orientation and planes commonly used to discuss and describe the human body. Your command of this vocabulary, and ability to use it appropriately, is necessary to effectively communicate your knowledge and understanding of the human skeleton. Additionally, bones, important features, and select landmarks are described and illustrated. Your ability to identify complete and fragmentary bones is a fundamental skill essential to the analysis of human remains, ensuring the accuracy of your results, interpretations, and conclusions.

## Learning Objectives

The laboratory projects presented in this chapter will facilitate your knowledge of the bones and important features of the human skeleton. During these exercises, you will learn those bones and skeletal features necessary to understand and apply the methods of analysis presented in the textbook and this lab manual.

## Expected Outcomes

By the end of this lab, you should be able to:

- Clearly define, describe, and illustrate the standard anatomical position, the anatomical planes, and the terms of orientation.
- Identify, by name, the major bones of the human skeleton in a complete and (if available) fragmentary condition.
- Identify, by name, select features on the bones of the human skeleton in both a complete and (if available) a fragmentary condition.

## Minimum Materials

An articulated human skeleton or good illustrations of an articulated human skeleton from different views
A disarticulated human skeleton or good illustrations of each bone of the human skeleton, including important features, from anterior, posterior, medial, and lateral views

## Optional Materials

Fragmentary human bones

## Basic Terms

Before beginning this exercise, review the section Overview of the Human Skeleton, especially Table 2.1 and Figure 2.1, in the textbook. You also may wish to review the following texts listed in the References: Bass (1995, 2005), Steele and Bramblett (1988), White and Folkens (1991, 1999), and White et al. (2012). Additionally, the osteology section of any anatomy textbook (e.g., *Gray's Anatomy*) has supplementary information. It is imperative that you understand and are able to use these terms during the lab sessions.

## Exercise 2.1: Cranial Skeleton

As mentioned in the textbook, the skull is composed of 22 outwardly visible bones, and three ossicles in each ear (which are not easily viewed). During this segment of the lab, you will identify most of these bones and some of their important features. Also, you will learn the names of the suture lines that separate the bones, as well as landmarks identified on the skull. Using Figures 2.2 through 2.6 in the textbook, take the lab skull and identify the following bones.

| | |
|---|---|
| Frontal | This bone comprises the forehead of humans as well as the upper eye orbits; two important features of this bone are the supraorbital tori (also called browridges) and the supraorbital margin (the upper margin of the eye orbits). |
| Zygomatic bones | These paired bones are the cheek bones that also form the lateral borders of the eye orbits and compose part of the zygomatic arch. |
| Lacrymals | These are the paired bones of the anterior, medial eye orbits. |
| Ethmoid | This is the complex bone at the rear of the eye orbits; this single bone comprises the posterior, medial walls of both eye orbits. |
| Nasals | These paired bones comprise the majority of the boney nose (i.e., the root and bridge). |
| Maxilla | These are the paired bones of the upper jaw that hold 16 of the 32 permanent teeth of the adult dentition. Together, they form the lower border of the nose and the nasal spine (if any). Observe the meeting of the nasal floor with the anterior maxilla; there may be a thin, vertical wall at this location. |
| Nasal conchae | These are the turbinated bones within the nose. |
| Vomer | This is the vertical bone that vertically divides the posterior nasal aperture in half. |
| Mandible | This is the lower jaw with its prominent (or not so prominent) chin (also called the mental eminence). Notice how it articulates with the skull at the temporal mandibular joint (TMJ) and how the dental arcade of this bone and that of the maxillae contact. |
| Palatines | These paired bones form the rear of the palate, posterior to the inferior maxillae. |
| Parietals | These are the paired bones of the superior braincase. |
| Occipital | This bone forms the posterior and inferior section of the braincase; features of note are the foramen magnum with its occipital condyles, and the roughened area on its inferioposterior surface for attachment of the neck muscles (the nuchal area). |
| Temporals | These are the paired bones of the inferior side of the braincase; the ear opening and mastoid process are important features of these bones. |
| Sphenoid | This very complex single bone separates the temporals and occipital from the other bones of the face. The so-called greater wing can be seen on the lateral side of the skull between the anterior temporal and the zygomatic bone. |

Now learn the suture lines of the skull. These are the special joints that connect the bones of the cranium (see Figures 2.8 through 2.12 in the textbook). The majority of these are named for the bones that they separate (e.g., the internasal suture separates the nasal bones). However, the following seven sutures have special names.
Coronal suture   This separates the frontal and parietals; it ends on either side at the point where the frontal meets the greater wing of the sphenoid.

| | |
|---|---|
| **Sagittal suture** | This suture separates the right and left parietal bones; it starts at the coronal suture and ends where the parietals meet the occipital. |
| **Lambdoid suture** | This separates the parietals from the occipital bone; it curves across the back of the skull, ending where the occipital and parietals meet the temporals. |
| **Squamosal suture** | This suture separates the superior portion of the temporals from the parietals. |
| **Incisive suture** | This suture separates that part of the maxillae that contain the incisors (called the premaxilla) from the rest of the bone. This is usually fused and invisible in adults. |
| **Transverse palatine suture** | This separates the maxillae from the palatines. |
| **Median palatine suture** | This separates the two maxillae and the two palatines in the palate. |

Finally, learn the major landmarks of the skull, which are depicted in Figures 2.8 through 2.12 in the textbook. The most important of these are:

| | |
|---|---|
| **Bregma** | The point where the sagittal suture meets anteriorly at the coronal suture in the sagittal plane. |
| **Basion** | The most inferior point on the anterior border of the foramen magnum. |
| **Nasion** | The point where the internasal suture (suture that separates the right from the left nasal bones) meets the nasofrontal suture in the midsagittal plane. |
| **Subnasale** | The point on the living that is roughly equivalent to a point below the lower margin of the nasal aperture in the midline. |
| **Glabella** | The most anterior point on the frontal in the midline; this point is located between the supraorbital tori (when present). |
| **Opisthocranion** | The farthest point on the back of the skull from glabella in the sagittal plane. |
| **Lambda** | The point where the sagittal and lambdoid sutures meet. |
| **Orale** | The point located in midsagittal plane where a line drawn across the posterior margins of the central incisors bisects the median palatine suture. |
| **Prosthion** | The most anterior point on the intermaxillary suture. |
| **Pterion** | The region where the greater wing of the sphenoid meets the frontal, parietal, and temporal. |
| **Obelion** | The point where a line drawn between the right and left parietal foramina bisects the sagittal suture. |
| **Ectocanthion** | The lateral most point on the lateral border of the eye. |
| **Asterion** | The point where the lambdoid suture meets the squamosal suture. |
| **Gnathion** | The lowest point on the mandible in the midline. |
| **Gonion** | The point where the ascending ramus meets the horizontal ramus. |
| **Zygoorbitale** | The point where the zygomaxillary suture contacts the lower border of the eye. |

Now, using Exercise Worksheets 2.1 A through 2.1 E, identify these bones, sutures, and landmarks on the five views of the skull. If you like, shade in each bone using a different color so that its boundaries are more easily distinguished.

## Exercise 2.2: Axial Skeleton

As described in the textbook, the axial skeleton is composed of the vertebral column, the rib cage, and the sternum. In this exercise, you will learn the basic units that make up these structures as well as features of the individual bones. Using Figure 2.16 in the textbook as a guide, take either a thoracic or a lumbar vertebra and try to identify the major features common to all of these bones:

| | |
|---|---|
| **Body** | The oval, boney segment that makes up the majority of the vertebra. |
| **Neural arch** | The complex part that arches posteriorly and creates the vertebral foramen. |
| **Spinous process** | That part of the neural arch that extends posteriorly and (usually) inferiorly. |
| **Transverse process** | Any one of several boney extensions that projects laterally from the right and left sides. |

Now, have the instructor give you one of each of the three types of vertebrae and, using the textbook's Figures 2.17 through 2.20, try to identify which one is cervical, thoracic, or lumbar. Also, ask to see the superior two bones of the axial skeleton: the atlas and axis. Finally, view the sacrum (Figure 2.31 of the textbook); try to distinguish the five vertebrae that are fused to form this bone. Test your knowledge by completing Exercise Worksheets 2.2 A and 2.2 B.

The rib cage is composed of 12 ribs that connect posteriorly to the vertebral column. Anteriorly, 10 of these are connected to the sternum through the costal cartilage; the 11th and 12th do not and, because of this, are called floating ribs. Each rib has two basic components (see Figure 2.21 in the textbook), the head and body. Have the lab instructor give you an assortment of ribs, and try to identify these two structures on the bones. Also, view the sternum (see Figure 2.15 in the textbook) and attempt to identify the joint between the manubrium and sternal body. Now, complete Exercise Worksheets 2.2 C and 2.2 D.

## Exercise 2.3: Appendicular Skeleton: Upper Limbs

The upper limb bones of the appendicular skeleton are the clavicle, scapula, humerus, ulna, radius, carpals (bones of the wrist), metacarpals (bones of the hand), and phalanges (bones of the fingers). In this exercise, you will concentrate on the first five of these bones; identification of the wrist, hand, and finger bones are beyond a lab of this nature. Before commencing this task, view Figures 2.22 through 2.26 in the textbook.

| | |
|---|---|
| Clavicle | This is the collarbone; it articulates medially with the manubrium of the sternum and laterally with the scapula. |
| Scapula | This is the shoulder blade; it has five important features: the spine, the glenoid cavity, the acromion, the coracoid process, and the ventral infraspinous plane. |
| Humerus | This is the upper bone of the arm; its major features are the head, the greater tuberosity, the lesser tuberosity, the deltoid tuberosity, the trochlea, and the olecranon fossa. |
| Ulna | This is the medial bone of the lower arm (when it is in the anatomical position); its major features are the olecranon process and the styloid process. |
| Radius | This is outside (lateral) bone of the lower arm; its major features are the head, the styloid process, the ulnar notch, and the radial tuberosity. |

Now complete Exercise Worksheets 2.3 A through 2.3 D; try to identify the bone pictured, and fill in each of the features indicated by an arrow.

## Exercise 2.4: Appendicular Skeleton: Lower Limbs

The lower limb bones of the appendicular skeleton are the os coxae, femur, tibia, patella, fibula, tarsals (bones of the ankle), metatarsals (bones of the foot), and phalanges (bones of the toes). In this exercise, you will concentrate on the first three of these bones; identification of the others is beyond a lab of this nature. View Figures 2.27, 2.28, 2.29, 2.30, 2.32, and 2.33 in the textbook before commencing this assignment.

| | |
|---|---|
| Os coxae | This bone is composed of three bones: the ilium, ischium, and pubis; important features of this bone are the greater sciatic notch, the pubic symphysis, the hip socket (called the acetabulum), the auricular surface, the preauricular sulcus, and the obturator foramen. |
| Femur | This is the thigh bone; its important features are the head, the greater and lesser trochanters, the linea aspera, the medial and lateral condyles, the intercondylar fossa, the supracondylar lines, and the popliteal surface. |
| Tibia | This is the main bone of the lower leg; its important features are the condyles, the intercondylar eminence, the tuberosity, the anterior crest, and the malleolus. |

Now complete Exercise Worksheets 2.4 A through 2.4 C; try to identify the bone pictured, and identify each of the features and cardinal directions indicated by an arrow.

## Exercise 2.5: Human Odontology

In this exercise, you will learn basic dental anatomy and recognize the types and placement of human teeth. Start by reviewing the anatomy of a tooth as illustrated in Figure 2.39 in the textbook. Now, look at the teeth provided by your lab instructor. Can you recognize the crown, with its white enamel and the peaks in the chewing surface (called cusps)? Now, locate the neck, and if you have been provided individual teeth (i.e., not situated in the maxillae or mandible), notice the root(s).

Now learn the six basic directions in the dentition. The first five are similar to the cardinal directions used in the body.

| | |
|---|---|
| **Mesial** | Toward the midline. |
| **Distal** | Away from the midline. |
| **Lingual** | Toward the tongue. |
| **Labial** | Toward the lips. |
| **Buccal** | Toward the cheeks. |
| **Occlusal** | The chewing surface of teeth. |

Next, learn the four quadrants of the mouth: upper left, upper right, lower left, and lower right. Within each of these, the sequence of teeth is the same; start mesially and work distally to learn the four basic types of teeth: incisors, canines, premolars, and molars (see Figure 2.40 of the textbook).

| | |
|---|---|
| **Incisors** | The flat, spatula-like teeth in the front of the mouth; these have a chisel-like edge without cusps. |
| **Canines** | The pointed teeth next to the second incisor; these are single-cusped teeth. |
| **Premolars** | The rectangular teeth next to the canine; these usually have two cusps, the labial one of which is often larger than its lingual counterpart. |
| **Molars** | The square or rectangular chewing teeth found at the rear of the mouth. |

Now complete Exercise Worksheet 2.5 by identifying the different teeth illustrated and the cardinal directions.

## NOTE TO INSTRUCTORS

Although real human skeletons are best for teaching osteology, their cost is too high for many schools. Plastic skeletons, either full or partial, usually are sufficient for an introductory class. These skeletons are available from Carolina Biological Supply (I have used these in my classes with good success) and the A. Daigger & Company, Inc. (see the section Sources of Materials at the beginning of this manual). Also, the bones of these skeletons should not be labeled, so students will have to identify each, and their concomitant features, using illustrations.

Because this is an introductory lab, not all of the 206 bones of the human skeleton are studied or pictured in the Exercise Worksheets. It is felt that a complete study of human osteology is beyond a lab of this nature. Instead, I concentrate on those bones that are used in later labs.

**Exercise Worksheet 2.1 A: Cranial Skeleton**

Name: _____ Date:_____

Identify the bones, cardinal directions (where indicated), features, landmarks, and sutures.

Cardinal direction: _____

Bone: _____

Bone: _____

Feature: _____

Landmark: _____

Feature: _____

Cardinal direction: _____

View (circle one):

| | |
|---|---|
| Anterior | Posterior |
| Superior | Inferior |
| Lateral | Medial |

**Exercise Worksheet 2.1 B: Cranial Skeleton**

Name: _____    Date:_____

Identify the bones, cardinal directions (where indicated), features, landmarks, and sutures.

Cardinal direction: _____

Bone: _____

Bone: _____

Suture: _____

Feature: _____

Landmark: _____

Landmark: _____

Bone: _____

Bone: _____

Suture: _____

Feature: _____

Bone: _____

Cardinal
direction: _____

View (circle one):

| Anterior | Posterior |
| Superior | Inferior |
| Lateral | Medial |

**Exercise Worksheet 2.1 C: Cranial Skeleton**

Name: _____    Date:_____

Identify the bones, cardinal directions (where indicated), features, landmarks, and sutures.

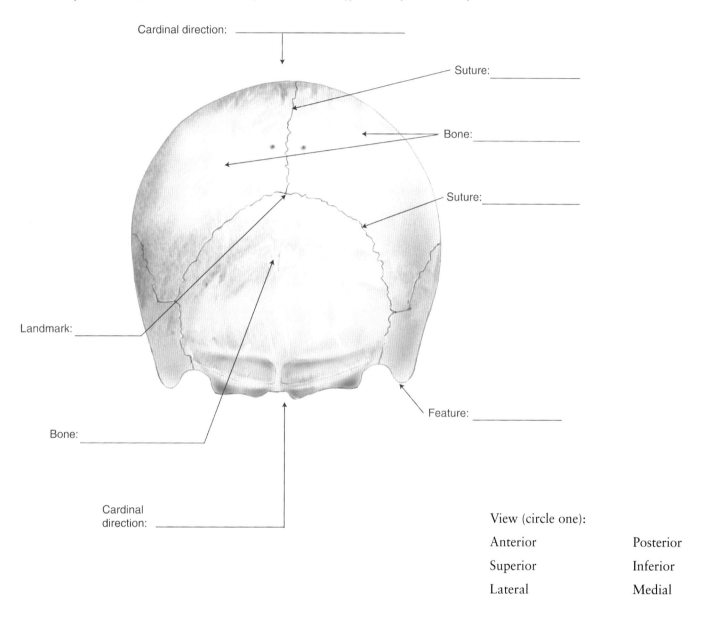

Cardinal direction: _____

Suture:_____

Bone:_____

Suture:_____

Landmark: _____

Bone: _____

Feature: _____

Cardinal
direction: _____

View (circle one):

| | |
|---|---|
| Anterior | Posterior |
| Superior | Inferior |
| Lateral | Medial |

**Exercise Worksheet 2.1 D: Cranial Skeleton**

Name: _____ Date:_____

Identify the bones, cardinal directions (where indicated), features, landmarks, and sutures.

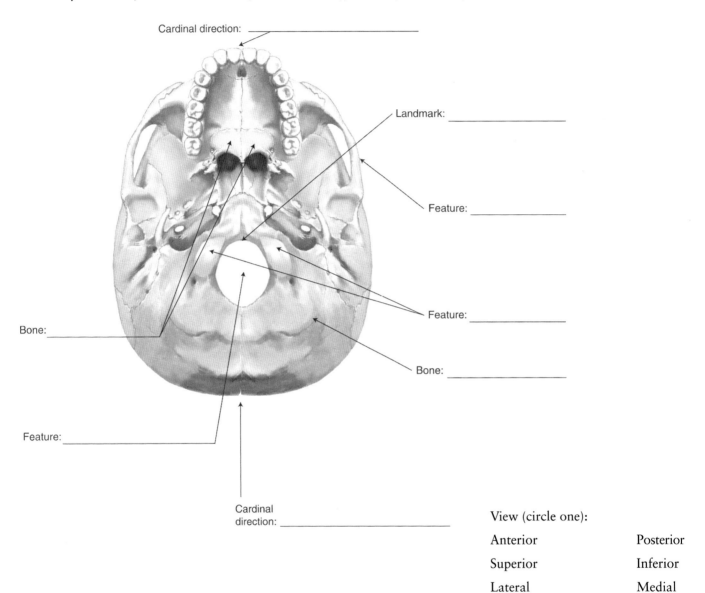

Cardinal direction: _____

Landmark: _____

Feature: _____

Feature: _____

Bone:

Bone: _____

Feature: _____

Cardinal direction: _____

View (circle one):

Anterior                Posterior

Superior                Inferior

Lateral                 Medial

## Exercise Worksheet 2.1 E: Cranial Skeleton

Name: _____    Date:_____

Identify the bones, cardinal directions (where indicated), features, landmarks, and sutures.

Cardinal direction: _____

Bone: _____

Landmark: _____

Suture: _____

Landmark: _____

Bone: _____

Bone: _____

Landmark: _____

Cardinal direction: _____

View (circle one):

Anterior          Posterior

Superior          Inferior

Lateral           Medial

**Exercise Worksheet 2.2 A: Axial Skeleton**

Name: _____  Date:_____

Identify the bones, cardinal directions, and bone features.

Cardinal direction: _____

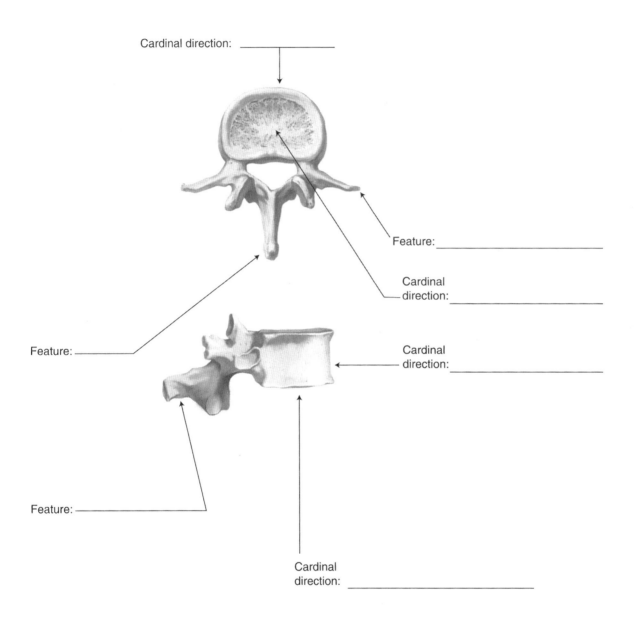

Feature: _____

Cardinal
direction: _____

Feature: _____

Cardinal
direction: _____

Feature: _____

Cardinal
direction: _____

Bone name: _____

**Exercise Worksheet 2.2 B: Axial Skeleton**

Name: _____    Date:_____

Identify the bone, cardinal directions, and bone features.

Cardinal direction: _____

Cardinal
direction: _____

Bone name: _____

View (circle one):

Anterior               Posterior

Superior               Inferior

Lateral                Medial

**Exercise Worksheet 2.2 C: Axial Skeleton**

Name: _____    Date:_____

Identify the bone and the indicated features.

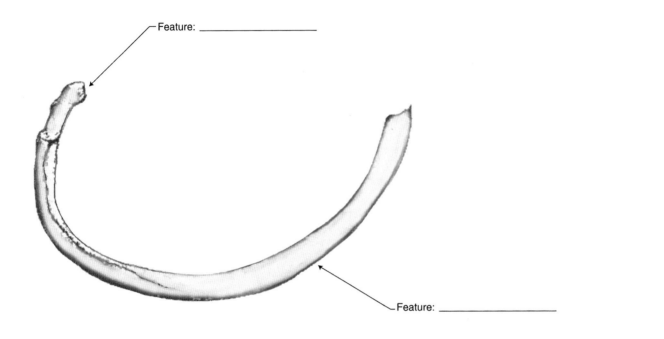

Feature: _____

Feature: _____

Bone name:_____

**Exercise Worksheet 2.2 D: Axial Skeleton**

Name: _____   Date:_____

Identify the bone, cardinal directions (where indicated), components, and features.

Cardinal
direction: _____

Feature: _____

Feature: _____

Cardinal
direction: _____

Bone name: _____

View (circle one):

Anterior                Posterior

Superior                Inferior

Lateral                 Medial

**Exercise Worksheet 2.3 A: Appendicular Skeleton: Upper Limbs**

Name: _____   Date:_____

Identify the bone, cardinal directions, and features.

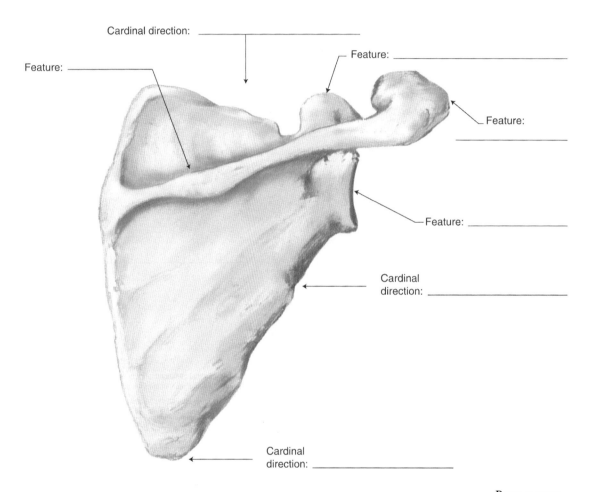

Cardinal direction: _____

Feature: _____

Feature: _____

Feature: _____
_____

Feature: _____

Cardinal direction: _____

Cardinal direction: _____

Bone name: _____

View (circle one):

| | |
|---|---|
| Anterior | Posterior |
| Superior | Inferior |
| Lateral | Medial |

**Exercise Worksheet 2.3 B: Appendicular Skeleton: Upper Limbs**

Name: _____   Date:_____

Identify the bone, cardinal directions, and features.

Cardinal direction: _____

Feature: _____

Feature: _____

Feature: _____

Feature: _____

Feature: _____

Cardinal
direction: _____

Bone name: _____

View (circle one):

| | |
|---|---|
| Anterior | Posterior |
| Superior | Inferior |
| Lateral | Medial |

Extra credit—Identify side (circle one):

Right            Left

## Exercise Worksheet 2.3 C: Appendicular Skeleton: Upper Limbs

Name: _____   Date:_____

Identify the bone, cardinal directions, and features.

Cardinal
direction: _____

Feature: _____

Feature: _____

Cardinal
direction: _____

Bone name: _____

View (circle one):

| | |
|---|---|
| Anterior | Posterior |
| Superior | Inferior |
| Lateral | Medial |

Extra credit—Identify side (circle one):

Right          Left

**Exercise Worksheet 2.3 D: Appendicular Skeleton: Upper Limbs**

Name: _____ Date: _____

Identify the bone, cardinal directions, and bone features.

Cardinal
direction: _____

Feature: _____

Feature: _____

Feature: _____

Feature: _____

Cardinal
direction: _____

Bone name: _____

View (circle one):

Anterior                           Posterior

Superior                           Inferior

Lateral                            Medial

Extra credit—Identify side (circle one):

Right                 Left

**Exercise Worksheet 2.4 A: Appendicular Skeleton: Lower Limbs**

Name: _____   Date: _____

Identify the bone, cardinal directions, and features.

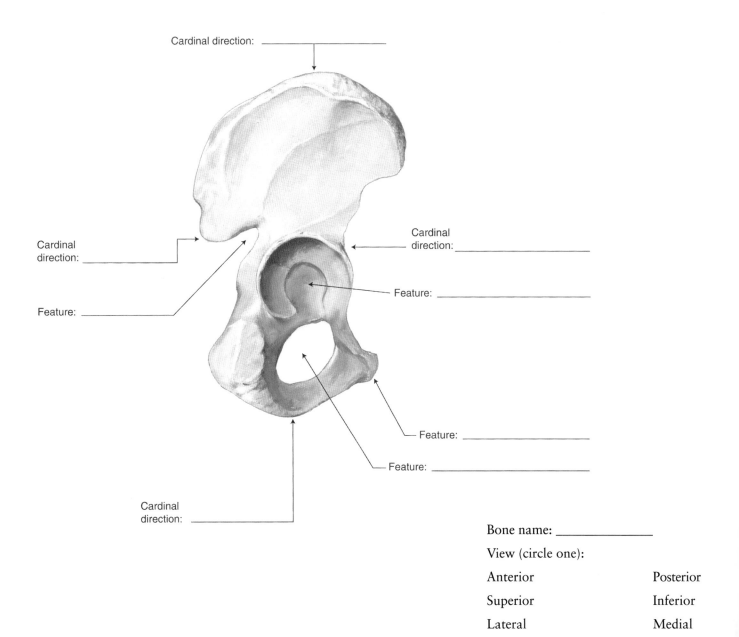

Cardinal direction: _____

Cardinal direction: _____

Cardinal direction: _____

Feature: _____

Feature: _____

Feature: _____

Feature: _____

Cardinal direction: _____

Bone name: _____

View (circle one):

Anterior                    Posterior

Superior                    Inferior

Lateral                     Medial


Extra credit—Identify side (circle one):

Right                Left

**Exercise Worksheet 2.4 B: Appendicular Skeleton: Lower Limbs**

Name: _____   Date:_____

Identify the bone, cardinal directions, and features.

Cardinal
direction: _____

Feature: _____

Feature: _____

Feature: _____

Feature: _____

Feature: _____

Feature: _____

Cardinal
direction: _____

Bone name: _____

Extra credit—Identify side (circle one):

Right          Left

View (circle one):

Anterior          Posterior

Superior          Inferior

Lateral          Medial

## Exercise Worksheet 2.4 C: Appendicular Skeleton: Lower Limbs

Name: _____    Date:_____

Identify the bone, cardinal directions, and features.

Cardinal direction: _____

Feature: _____

Feature: _____

Feature: _____

Feature: _____

Feature: _____

Cardinal direction: _____

Bone name: _____

View (circle one):

Anterior                          Posterior

Superior                          Inferior

Lateral                            Medial

Extra credit—Identify side (circle one):

Right                    Left

**Exercise Worksheet 2.5: Human Odontology**

Name: _____   Date:_____

Identify the teeth and the cardinal directions.

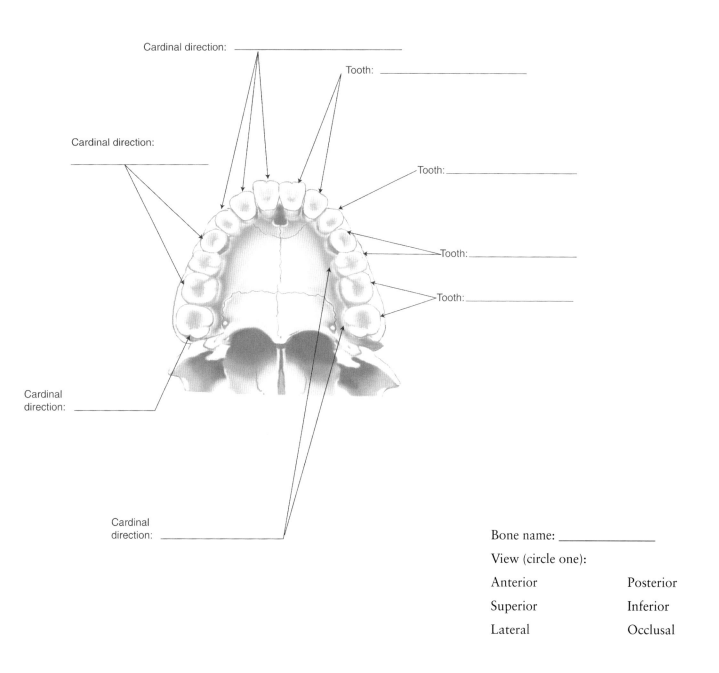

Cardinal direction: _____

Tooth: _____

Cardinal direction:

_____

Tooth:_____

Tooth:_____

Tooth:_____

Cardinal
direction: _____

Cardinal
direction: _____

Bone name: _____

View (circle one):

Anterior                Posterior

Superior               Inferior

Lateral                  Occlusal

# 3   Establishing Medicolegal Significance

As discussed in the textbook, the first issue usually faced by forensic anthropologists involves recognizing the forensic significance of osteological material. This involves three separate tasks: (1) distinguishing bone from nonbone, (2) differentiating human from nonhuman bone, and (3) discerning recent from old bone. If your lab has the necessary material, each of these steps should be performed in this order. This is only logical; after all, why try to identify the bone from which a fragment may have originated when the fragment is not even bone? Similarly, why spend time determining the age (i.e., contemporary versus noncontemporary) of a bone if it is not even human? Before continuing, read Chapter 3 in the textbook to familiarize yourself with the methods used for establishing medicolegal significance.

## Learning Objectives

The purpose of this lab is to provide you with information needed to distinguish bone from nonbone, human bone from nonhuman bone, and contemporary from noncontemporary osteological remains.

## Expected Outcomes

By the end of this lab, you should be able to:

- Recognize the characteristics of bone when viewed under a microscope, and be able to distinguish this material from other substances that can appear to be osteological material.
- Distinguish human from the most commonly seen nonhuman bones (e.g., mammals) based on the size and configuration of the remains. This includes separating subadult humans from small nonhuman animals, and adult humans from large mammals and other creatures.
- Recognize those features of human bone that identify it as relatively young (i.e., having died within the last 50 years) as opposed to human bone that is older (in many cases, much older) than 50 years.

## BONE AND TEETH VERSUS OTHER MATERIAL EXERCISE

### Minimum Materials

Assorted human or nonhuman bones and teeth and/or bone and tooth fragments
Standard laboratory microscope
Various bone-like materials (e.g., wood, shell, nutshell, pottery)

## HUMAN VERSUS NONHUMAN EXERCISE

### Minimum Materials

Adult human bones (real or plastic)
Nonhuman bones (real or plastic)

## Optional Materials

Subadult human bones (real or plastic)
Reference works on nonhuman animals (e.g., Cornwall, 1956; Gilbert, 1973; Gilbert et al., 1981; Schmid, 1972)

## CONTEMPORARY VERSUS NONCONTEMPORARY EXERCISE

## Minimum Materials

Modern bones of any kind, human or nonhuman
Ancient bones (e.g., over 100 years old), human or nonhuman

## Optional Materials

Prehistoric human bones with dental, cranial, or other modification
Modern human bones and teeth with cultural modifications (e.g., amalgams, surgical implants)

## Exercise 3.1: Distinguishing Bone and Teeth From Other Material

As described in the textbook, Douglas Ubelaker (1998) was one of the first forensic anthropologists to point out the value of microscopic analysis in distinguishing bone from nonosteological material. Although methods using microscopy can be very complex (e.g., determining the chemical makeup of a sample using the Spectral Library for Identification and Classification Explorer [SLICE] at the FBI laboratory in Washington, D.C.), bone and teeth can be distinguished from other material in cases of extreme fragmentation simply by viewing it under a standard laboratory microscope. When magnified, bone will reveal a fairly compact surface with some graininess (especially in the old). However, fibrous materials and complex-layered structures filled with cell-like openings are not expected. If your laboratory has a microscope, examine various materials under different powers. Notice the ivory-like appearance of bone that is only duplicated in pottery and similar substances. Notice also that materials such as wood and other plant remains do not have the compact look of bone, but show fibrous structures and layering. When viewing fragmented teeth, remember that the dentin is similar to bone, while the white color and smooth surface of tooth enamel is not replicated in other osteological structures.

Now, take the material of unknown nature supplied by the lab instructor. In Exercise Worksheet 3.1, describe the surface of the sample in as much detail as you can. Include such items as surface contour, presence of openings, color, layering, and compactness. After this, make your determination as to bone or nonbone in the area provided, and justify your answer.

## Exercise 3.2: Distinguishing Human From Nonhuman Remains

As described in the textbook, there are two aspects of bones that help in making the distinction between human and nonhuman remains: maturity and architecture. Maturity refers to the unfused or missing epiphyses on various ends and other parts of bone; understanding this is crucial to distinguishing the bone of human subadults from the nonhuman bone of smaller animals, especially mammals. Architecture, which refers to the shape of the bones, is necessary to understand the differences between the bones of adult humans and those of large animals (e.g., deer, cows).

### *Subadult Humans Versus Small Adult Animals*

To distinguish humans from nonhumans, view the ends of the bones of both immature human and adult nonhuman animals. Notice the lack of epiphyses (or at least separation of these from their respective bones), with their smooth articular surfaces, on the subadult humans, while these structures are visibly fused in the adult nonhumans. Also, in some osteological structures, bones that are normally joined (e.g., os coxa) are separate in subadult humans, while they are composed of fused bone in adult nonhumans.

### Adult Humans Versus Adult, Large Animals

As mentioned in the textbook, architectural (shape) differences are the main method for distinguishing human from nonhuman bones of equal size. Using Figures 3.7 and 3.8 of the textbook, start with the skull; notice the large braincase with small face and absence of a prominent snout that characterizes the human skull. Now notice how, in the other animals, the snout is larger and more projecting and the braincase is smaller. Additionally, if present, the projecting saber-like teeth on any carnivore skull helps distinguish felines and canines from humans.

Next, move to the axial skeleton and thorax. Starting with the vertebral column, notice the differences between the vertebrae of a nonhuman from those of a human (refer to Figures 2.17 through 2.20 of the textbook for views of these bones in humans). Notice that the vertebrae of most nonhuman animals have longer spinous processes than seen in the human (see Figure 3.1 in this manual). Notice also that the shape of the neck vertebrae can be significantly different in quadrupeds, such as sheep and cows, when compared with these same bones in humans (see Figure 3.1 in this manual). Moving to the thorax, notice the difference in the amount of curvature of the ribs of humans when compared with nonhumans. The former are almost in the shape of the letter "C," while the latter are more straight (Figure 3.11a of the textbook). Finally, observe the differences in the shape of the sternum; those of quadrupeds are parallel-sided and taper at each end, while the human counterpart is wide and flat at the superior end (the manubrium) but narrow and rounded inferiorly (Figure 3.11b of the textbook), giving it an overall T-shape.

Moving to the bones of the upper limbs of the appendicular skeleton (see Figures 3.12 through 3.14 of the textbook), notice that the scapula of humans is widest near the glenoid fossa, while it is widest away from this structure in nonhumans (see Figure 3.2 in this manual). The humerus of humans differs from those of other animals in a similar manner for all long limb bones: For a given length, the human limb bone is more slender than that of nonhuman animals. In addition to this difference, the greater tubercle on the proximal end is small and nonprojecting in humans, while it is long and hook-shaped in many quadrupeds (see Figure 3.3 in this manual). The lower bones of the upper (front) limbs, the radius and ulna, are distinct in humans in that they are separate; in other animals, these bones are often fused in the area equivalent to the human wrist. Finally, the metacarpals and metatarsals, called the

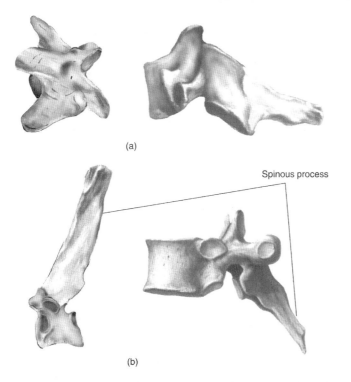

*Figure 3.1* Vertebrae of human and nonhuman: (**a**) lateral view of cervical vertebrae of wolf (*left*) and human (*right*); (**b**) thoracic vertebrae of wolf (*left*) and human (*right*); notice the different configuration of the cervical vertebrae and long spinous process on the thoracic vertebrae of the wolf.

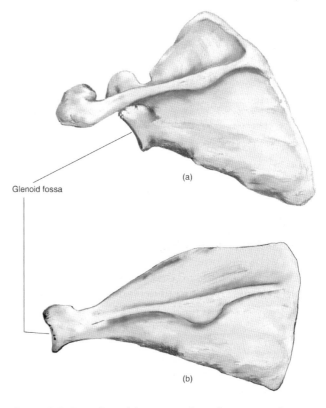

*Figure 3.2* Scapulae of human and nonhuman: (**a**) human; (**b**) pig; notice the placement of the glenoid fossa in relation to the widest part of the bone.

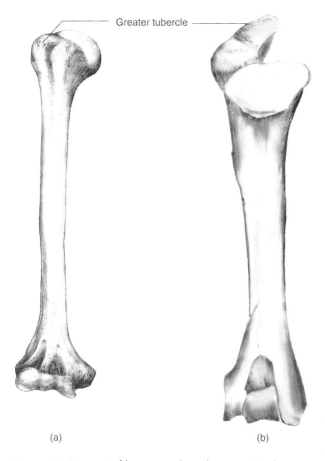

Greater tubercle

(a)    (b)

*Figure 3.3* Humeri of human and nonhuman: (**a**)   human; (**b**) elk; notice the hook-like greater tubercle on the bone of the elk.

**metapodials,** of nonhuman animals are single, long, and slender bones that are easily distinguished from the multiple bones of the human hand (and foot).

Now, view the bones of the lower limbs of the appendicular skeleton (Figures 3.15 through 3.17 of the textbook). The human os coxa is distinctive in being short and wide when compared to the long and narrow shape of this bone in the quadruped. Also, the triangular shape of the pubis and ischium in humans distinguishes these bones from the almost square appearance of their counterparts in quadrupeds. For the other bone of the pelvis, the sacrum, the task of distinguishing human from nonhuman is relatively easy. In humans, this structure is somewhat triangular in outline, while this set of fused bones is more T-shaped in nonhumans (see Figure 3.10 of the textbook). Turning to the lower or rear limbs, the femora of humans can be distinguished from other animals by the long, slender shape of the bone with its long neck (that well separates the head from the shaft) and shortness of the greater trochanter. In quadrupeds, this bone is thicker in comparison to its length. In addition, the neck is not as distinctive, and the greater trochanter projects superiorly to the head (see Figure 3.4 in this manual). Finally, notice that the distal articular surface of the femur continues higher on the shaft of the ungulates than it does on humans. The differences in the tibia are similar to those of the femur and other long limb bones; that is, humans' are thin by comparison to those of the same lengths in nonhumans. Also, notice the multiple notches at the distal ends of the ungulates, and the larger and more projecting tuberosity on quadrupeds when compared to humans (see Figure 3.5 in this manual).

Now, using Exercise Worksheet 3.2, analyze the lab specimen given to you by the instructor to determine if it is human or nonhuman. Use the table provided on the worksheet as a decision matrix (see the section in Chapter 1 of the textbook for a description) to aid you in this task. When complete, circle the appropriate decision (i.e., human or nonhuman) and provide any justification for your conclusion in the comments section.

### Exercise 3.3: Distinguishing Contemporary From Noncontemporary Remains

As described in the textbook, there are four aspects that help distinguish medicolegally significant (i.e., contemporary) remains from those that are not: state of preservation, body modification, personal belongings, and conditions of interment. In this lab, an exercise is presented only for the first two aspects since the last two are most often evident at the time of body recovery. Thus, you will need to learn those aspects of bone and teeth that involve distinguishing contemporary from noncontemporary osteological remains based on the state of preservation and cultural modifications.

As noted in the textbook, there are seven traits of preservation that help distinguish contemporary from noncontemporary remains: color, texture, hydration, weight, condition, fragility, and amount of soft tissue. Try to assess each of these in the lab specimen. Is the bone's color white, somewhat off-white, tan, or brown? How about the texture of its surface? Is it smooth like ivory, or grainy and pitted? How about its moisture content? Does it have a moist and greasy look and feel, or is it dry and porous? Now try to determine its weight. Does it seem heavy for its size, or relatively light as though it were made of heavy Styrofoam? How about the overall condition of the bone? Is it fragmentary or all in one piece? Now try to gauge the toughness of bone. Does it seem strong and capable of withstanding some stress (e.g., being dropped without breaking), or does it seem fragile and ready to break merely by handling? Finally, is there any soft tissue present, and if so, is it very dry?

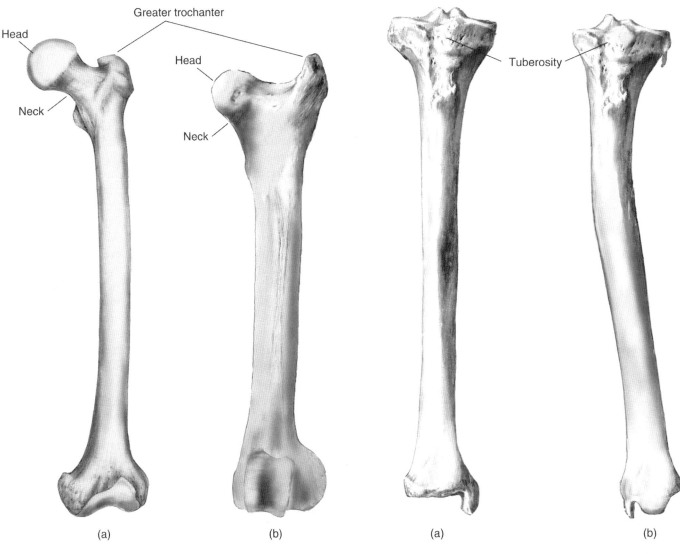

*Figure 3.4* Femora of human and nonhuman: **(a)** human; **(b)** elk; notice that the elk has a more superior projection of the greater trochanter and the neck and head merge more than in the human.

*Figure 3.5* Tibiae of human and nonhuman: **(a)** human; **(b)** elk; notice the larger tuberosity and the greater contour of the distal end of the elk.

Since it is common for people in all societies to modify their bodies in some manner, you should make a visual assessment to determine if the lab specimen exhibits any cultural alterations. Start by viewing the skull (if present) to see if it displays cranial deformation. If present, this will be obvious by the loss of rounding on the anterior or posterior bones of the braincase. Next, view the dentition. If there is evidence that the teeth were filed to points or other shapes (see Figure 3.22 in the textbook), then the teeth are probably prehistoric. However, the presence of amalgams (fillings), caps, bridges, false teeth, and other such appliances is more indicative of contemporary remains. Finally, view the postcranial bones for prosthetics such as plates, hip replacements, and other implants. Their presence indicates that the remains are contemporary.

Now, use the table in Exercise Worksheet 3.3 as a decision matrix (see Chapter 1 in the textbook for a description) to determine the medicolegal significance of the lab specimen. In the matrixes, circle the word in each row that best fits what is seen in the bones and teeth. Once completed, count the circles in each column, and enter the value on the total count line. Reviewing all of your findings, decide on the most likely "age" of the skeletal material, and circle the appropriate word (i.e., either *Noncontemporary* or *Contemporary*). Also, if other information needs to be provided, write it in the comments area.

## NOTE TO INSTRUCTORS

Some materials for this lab can be obtained from multiple sources. Nonbone substances are available simply by getting weathered materials from outside; a walk through a field may provide enough objects that look like bone fragments. Casts of nonhuman bones are available from the sources listed in the Source of Materials section of this manual. However, a butcher shop or a pet store may have the long limb bones of cows that would be useful for this lab. In addition, fresh bones from a butcher shop can illustrate how fresh human bone appears. If you can acquire prehistoric bones, they will often be Native American remains; be sensitive to the feelings of local tribes when using these in a lab of this kind.

**Exercise Worksheet 3.1: Distinguishing Bone and Teeth From Other Material**

Name: _____   Date: _____

Case/Accession number: _____

Description: _____

_____

_____

_____

Decision (circle one):        Bone        Nonbone

Justification: _____

_____

_____

_____

**Exercise Worksheet 3.2: Distinguishing Human From Nonhuman Remains**

Name: _____   Date: _____

Case/Accession number: _____

| *Bone* | *Human* | *Nonhuman* |
|---|---|---|
| Skull | | |
|    Braincase | Large | Small |
|    Snout | Small | Large |
|    Canine teeth | Nonprojecting | Projecting |
| Vertebrae | | |
|    Spinous processes | Small | Large |
| Thorax | | |
|    Ribs | C-shaped | Curved |
|    Sternum | | |
|       Body ends | Rounded | Tapered |
|       Overall shape | T-shaped | Parallel-sided |
| Upper limb bones | | |
|    Scapula—widest part | At glenoid | Away from glenoid |
|    Humerus | | |
|       Robusticity | Thin | Heavy |
|       Greater trochanter | Short | Projecting |
|    Radius and ulna | Separate | Fused |
|    Metacarpals | 5 | 1 |

| Bone | Human | Nonhuman |
|---|---|---|
| Lower limb bones | | |
| Os coxa | | |
| Shape | Short and wide | Long and narrow |
| Ischium and pubis shape | Triangular | Square |
| Femur | | |
| Robusticity | Thin | Heavy |
| Greater trochanter | Short | Projecting |
| Tibia | | |
| Robusticity | Thin | Heavy |
| Distal surface | Simple | Complex |
| Metatarsals | 5 | 1 |
| **Total count** | | |

Decision (circle one):      Human       Nonbone

Comments: _____

_____

_____

_____

**Exercise Worksheet 3.3: Distinguishing Noncontemporary From Contemporary Remains**

Name: _____ Date: _____

Case/Accession number: _____

### State of Preservation

| Characteristic | Noncontemporary | Contemporary |
|---|---|---|
| Color | Dark | Light |
| Surface texture | Grainy | Smooth |
| Hydration | Dry | Wet, greasy |
| Weight | Light | Heavy |
| Condition | Fragmented | Whole |
| Fragility | Fragile | Tough |
| Soft tissue | Absent | Present |
| **Total count** | | |

### Body Modifications

| Characteristic | Noncontemporary | Contemporary |
|---|---|---|
| **Teeth** | | |
| Filing | Present | Absent |
| Amalgams | Absent | Present |
| Bridges | Absent | Present |
| Caps | Absent | Present |
| False teeth | Absent | Present |

| Characteristic | Noncontemporary | Contemporary |
|---|---|---|
| Skull | | |
| Deformation | Present | Absent |
| Surgical implants | Absent | Present |
| Postcranium | | |
| Surgical implants | Absent | Present |
| Surgical modifications | Absent | Present |
| **Total count** | | |

Decision (circle one):       Noncontemporary        Contemporary

**Comments:** _____

_____

_____

_____

# 4  Recovery Scene Methods

The involvement of the forensic anthropologist as soon as decomposed or skeletonized remains are located is crucial to the thorough and well-documented recovery of human remains and associated evidence. It is a well-known adage that forensic science begins at the crime scene and that poorly processed crime scenes will adversely affect the quality of all subsequent evidentiary analyses and (possibly) the admissibility of evidence. With this in mind, a forensic anthropologist brings to the crime scene investigation a set of specialized skills necessary to effectively process this type of evidence. The forensic anthropologist's in-depth knowledge of the human skeleton, and the ability to identify human bone in a fragmented condition, results in a more complete recovery of the remains. The forensic anthropologist can offer continual on-scene feedback about, for example, whether the remains are human or nonhuman, whether there are missing elements, and what is the minimum number of individuals involved. Additionally, most forensic anthropologists are well trained in archaeological field methods, and can assist in the recovery of remains and document the crime scene to facilitate accurate reconstruction of events. Finally, they are well aware of packaging practices that reduce damage and commingling of remains.

Before beginning the projects detailed in this chapter, review Chapter 4 in the textbook. The laboratory sessions presented here build toward the final assignment, an in-depth crime scene investigation of a surface-deposited body. The first session prepares students for the most time-consuming activity: documentation through mapping, photography, and note taking.

## Learning Objectives

During this lab, you will learn the basic skills of setting up a grid over a mock recovery scene, mapping a small scatter of evidence, photographing relevant materials, and evidence packaging. Additionally, you will learn how to locate human remains, document the recovery scene, and collect and package evidence. Finally, you will learn how to excavate an interred body.

## Expected Outcomes

By the end of this lab, you should be able to:

- Establish a grid using a compass and measuring tapes.
- Produce an accurate map of a recovery scene.
- Complete an evidence log listing all items encountered with assigned numbers.
- Complete a photographic log listing a summary of photos necessary to thoroughly represent the scene as you encountered it.
- Collect human remains while maintaining the chain of evidence.
- Excavate an interred body using forensic archaeological methods.

## Minimum Materials

### Exercise 4.1

Each group (students should be divided into groups) will need all of the materials listed here, which can be organized into a kit. A garden caddy is a useful container for the necessary materials:

Clipboard
Graph paper

Evidence log
Photo log
Chain of custody/Evidence transfer form
Pencils
Straight edge
Sharpie markers
2 measuring implements such as yard sticks, tape measures, or folding carpenter's rulers
Index cards cut into small squares to serve as evidence numbers
Plastic/paper bags
Evidence tape or clear packing tape
3 clipboards (one for the photographer to record photos taken, one for the person recording the assigned evidence numbers, and one for the person responsible for the map)
Wooden stakes to form the corners of the grid (if exercise is being done outdoors)
Pin flags of 3 colors: 1 for the grid, 1 for the associated physical evidence, 1 for the human remains (if exercise is being done outdoors)
String
Calculator
Cardboard boxes (to transport the evidence in)

A "scene" consisting of 12–18 pieces of evidence (several human bones, bone fragments, and associated evidence)

### *Exercise 4.2*

All of the materials in Exercise 4.1 with the following additions:

Shovel
Screen(s) (¼ inch and ⅛ inch)
Brush
Trowel
Interred body (plastic skeleton recommended)

## Optional Materials

A camera for each team (disposable, 35 mm, or digital)
Film or a CD for photographs
A video camera for each team
A video cassette
Photo scales (ABFO No. 2 scale is useful, or a simple ruler will suffice)
Metal detector

## Exercise 4.1: Surface-Deposited Body (Outdoor or Indoor)

This laboratory session involves a simulated crime scene investigation. The class will work in groups to locate and process a scene consisting of surface-deposited human remains and associated physical evidence. Activities required include organizing team members and assigning each individual team member specific scene responsibilities, conducting a systematic search for the human remains and associated physical evidence, recovering relevant evidence and human remains, thoroughly documenting (through note taking, photography, videotaping, and mapping) the investigation and findings, and submitting a formal report that summarizes the crime scene processing and findings.

Use the following protocol to process this scene:

1. Chief investigative officer (Lab Instructor) reviews the scene and determines the best route of entrance and exit. (At a real scene, this person also arranges for securing the scene and posts personnel to maintain security.)
2. Take photographs and videotape environmental setting, landscape, surrounding landmarks, and so on; record in the photo log.

3. Walk the area in regular intervals in order to identify location and nature of evidence. *Flag* each piece of evidence encountered, and *assign a number* to it. Evidence should be numbered sequentially in order of discovery. Use different-colored or -shaped flags for human remains and physical evidence. *All flagged evidence should be entered into the evidence log and photographed.*
4. Once all evidence has been flagged, additional photographs should be taken, including the overall scene from location of the body and close-ups of each piece of evidence in situ (including human remains). All photographs should be recorded in the photo log and be taken with and without a scale.
5. Determine datum and establish coordinates of permanent datum.
6. Establish a grid over the area of greatest concentration of human remains. Set corners first using triangulation technique (Pythagorean theorem: $A^2 + B^2 = C^2$), mark at regular intervals (e.g., every 2 feet) along two of the parallel sides with flags, mark intervals along the adjacent sides with flags. Define interior units by stringing between opposite and adjacent pin flags.
7. Remove all vegetation and other debris covering the remains (if done outdoors) in order to get a clear view of the position and association of the remains (if done outdoors) and any associated evidence; photograph in situ.
8. Map the location of the body and associated evidence; include information on the physical environment. Mapping should be done in pencil and include the following information: a scale, a north arrow, date, case number, recorder, a legend, site location, county, state, evidence numbers, and any additional comments.
9. Bag each piece of evidence. The information on the bag should include date, case number, general site location, county, state, evidence number, general description of the item in the bag, number of items in the bag, and name of the investigator (student). The evidence bag should be sealed properly and initialed.
10. During the entire scene investigation, make notes on methods, activities, nature of evidence, nature of scene, general environment, weather, and body position. Be exhaustive—too much is better than too little. Write further notes following investigation if necessary and relevant. Never hurry through the investigation of a scene.

## Exercise 4.2: Interred Body (Outdoor)

Retrieving all relevant information from interments requires the controlled excavation of the remains following the methods of forensic archaeology. After all surface findings over the grave are located, mapped, and collected, establish a grid square and attach a line level to the grid strings so that the vertical, as well as horizontal, location of items within the grave can be determined. Remove the dirt within, or immediately around, the burial pit by skimming it carefully from the surface (see Figure 4.9 in the textbook) until the human remains are encountered (most frequently the pelvis or foot). As you remove the dirt 1 to 2 inches at a time, use a metal detector (if available) to scan below the level being excavated. As items are encountered, they should be fully uncovered but left in place (see Figure 4.10 in the textbook) for mapping, recording, and photographing. If the excavation goes deeper than 8 inches, sacrifice one wall of the grave by digging down alongside the burial pit, to the level of the burial, to allow access to the remains.

Once part of the body has been located, uncover the remains but do not remove them until they are fully exposed, mapped, and photographed. For this part, small trowels or digging sticks should be used to remove overlying dirt (see Figure 4.11a in the textbook), with the additional use of brushes (see Figure 4.11b in the textbook) except when clothing or other fibers are present.

As soil is moved out of the grave, sift it through a 1/4-inch or finer screen (see Figure 4.12a of the textbook) to recover small objects (Figure 4.12b of the textbook). Although tedious, valuable information is gained by taking the time to sift grave fill dirt. In addition to dry sifting, dirt can be washed through the screen to help reveal fragments of evidence.

## NOTE TO INSTRUCTORS

This lab is a favorite among students. I have set up simulated forensic sites using plastic or real human bones and weathered materials such as shotgun shell casings, old clothing (left outside), beer bottles, and soda cans. After assembling the materials, find an area on campus where student use is not high (although visibility will help "sell" this class to the student body) and lay out the remains in a scattered or (if desired) organized pattern.

This is one of the more complex projects presented in this manual, and it involves a great deal of planning on your part, as well as student preparation. It takes approximately 2–3 hours to complete, depending on the size of the mock scene and the number of human remains and physical evidence present. I offer the following suggestions to facilitate an organized, smooth lab session that will enhance the student experience.

1.  During the class session preceding this lab, provide time for students to assemble their teams (ideally composed of four to six people), identify and discuss the different tasks that must be accomplished during the scene investigation, and define the responsibilities of each team member. This is also a good time to assign each team a case number and go over the forms they will be filling out, as well as demonstrate how to use equipment such as cameras and video cameras.

2.  Prepare each kit with the necessary materials before the lab begins and go over the materials and equipment in the kit with the student. This informs the students about what is in the kit and how to use the equipment while saving time in "the field" and again helps students to more efficiently conduct the scene investigation.

3.  Allow time during the class session following the lab for student discussion of the experience: what went well, what was problematic, and how well the team worked together. Review the situations that arose that required a decision to be made and how it was made. Also, discuss with them the format of the report they will be submitting. I have included an example of a grade sheet for this assignment that defines the criteria to assign the group grade.

4.  Extra "evidence" can be secured from many sources. I have walked in the mesa areas around Albuquerque for items such as beer bottles, coke cans, and discarded shell casings. These types of finds add authenticity to your lab. I recommend keeping a list of your objects so that nothing is accidentally left outside after the lab is over.

5.  If it is inconvenient to perform this lab outdoors, students respond well to a simulated scene indoors. I have set up an "outdoor" scene in an empty classroom with positive results.

**Exercise Worksheet 4.1 A: Surface-Deposited Body (Outdoor or Indoor)**

### Evidence/Bag Log

Name: _____ Date: _____

Case/Accession number: _____

| Bag number | Evidence number | Description of contents |
|---|---|---|
| | | |
| | | |
| | | |
| | | |
| | | |
| | | |
| | | |
| | | |
| | | |
| | | |
| | | |
| | | |
| | | |
| | | |

Total number of evidence bags: _____

Total number of boxes for evidence transport: _____

Recovery team members: _____

_____

_____

Comments: _____

_____

_____

_____

**Exercise Worksheet 4.1 B: Surface-Deposited Body (Outdoor or Indoor)**

## Photo Log

Name: _____ Date: _____

Case/Accession number: _____

Film roll _____ of _____

Film type (circle one):       B/W prints     Color prints   Slides

Camera type (circle one):    Digital       Manual      Automatic    Polaroid

| Photo number | View | Description |
|---|---|---|
| | | |
| | | |
| | | |
| | | |
| | | |
| | | |
| | | |
| | | |
| | | |
| | | |
| | | |
| | | |
| | | |
| | | |

Comments: _____

_____

_____

_____

Exercise Worksheet 4.1 C: Surface-Deposited Body (Outdoor or Indoor)

**Mapping of Scene**

Name: _____ Date: _____

Case/Accession number: _____

Scale: _____

**Exercise Worksheet 4.2 A: Interred Body (Outdoor)**

### Evidence/Bag Log

Name: _____ Date: _____

Case/Accession number: _____

| Bag number | Evidence number | Description of contents |
|---|---|---|
| | | |
| | | |
| | | |
| | | |
| | | |
| | | |
| | | |
| | | |
| | | |
| | | |
| | | |
| | | |
| | | |

Total number of evidence bags: _____

Total number of boxes for evidence transport: _____

Recovery team members: _____

_____

_____

Comments: _____

_____

_____

_____

**Exercise Worksheet 4.2 B: Interred Body (Outdoor)**

## Photo Log

Name: _____ Date: _____

Case/Accession number: _____

Film roll _____ of _____

| | | | |
|---|---|---|---|
| **Film type (circle one):** | B/W prints | Color prints | Slides |
| **Camera type (circle one):** | Digital | Manual | Automatic | Polaroid |

| *Photo number* | *View* | *Description* |
|---|---|---|
| | | |
| | | |
| | | |
| | | |
| | | |
| | | |
| | | |
| | | |
| | | |
| | | |
| | | |
| | | |
| | | |

Comments: _____

_____

_____

_____

**Exercise Worksheet 4.2 C: Interred Body (Outdoor)**

**Mapping of Scene**

Name: _____ Date: _____

Case/Accession number: _____

Scale: _____

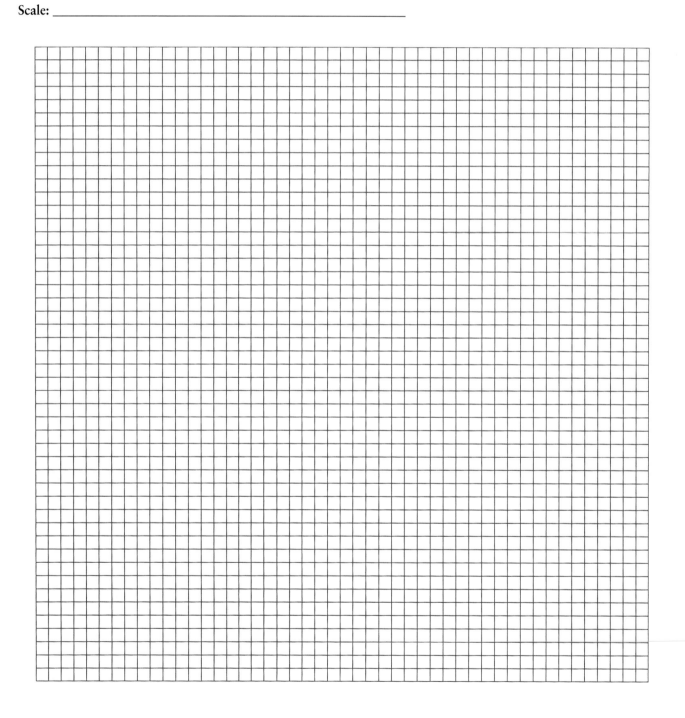

# 5 Estimating Postmortem Interval

With the discovery of human remains, the estimation of postmortem interval (PMI) is one of the factors used by law enforcement authorities to examine missing persons' files in search of a likely match. Therefore, its accurate determination may make the difference between the eventual identification of the deceased or an unclaimed body. This chapter will allow you to explore three methods for estimating this parameter: decomposition, animal scavenging, and deterioration of accompanying money and clothing. As with the other labs, it is imperative that you read the accompanying chapter in the textbook before commencing the exercises given here.

## Learning Objectives

The purpose of this lab is to acquaint you with the methods for assigning time since death based on the outward appearance of decedents and the material goods recovered with them.

## Expected Outcomes

By the end of this lab, you should be able to:

- Estimate PMI (also known as time since death) based on the general amount of decomposition of human bodies.
- Estimate PMI based on Total Aquatic Decomposition Score (TADS) and Accumulated Degree Days (ADD) for decomposed human bodies discovered in an aquatic environment (e.g., lake, river).
- Estimate PMI based on the amount of animal scavenging.
- Estimate PMI based on the general deterioration of clothing and paper money.

## Minimum Materials

Photographs of decomposed bodies
Photographs of bodies scavenged by animals

## Optional Materials

Deteriorated clothing and paper money

## Exercise 5.1: Estimating PMI Using General Decomposition

Commence this lab by familiarizing yourself with the various changes that occur during decomposition in the three basic climates of North America discussed in the textbook (see Tables 5.1, 5.2, 5.3, and 5.4 in this manual). Notice the similarity in the phases in the different climates. Insect activity and skin discoloration are common in the earlier stages of decomposition, while sagging flesh with eventual exposure of bone is seen in the middle stages, and bleaching accompanied by cracking and loss of cortical bone are seen in the latter stages.

Now, view the photographs provided by your instructor. If skin is present and the photo is in color, is it discolored or the color of human flesh (pay attention to the ancestral background)? If skin in present, is the body bloated or deflated? Is there caving of the abdominal cavity? Does the skin look flexible or dry and papery? If bone is showing, how much of the skeleton is visible? Less than half? Over half? Does the surface of the bone look clean and dry, or wet and greasy? Does the bone show bleaching? Flaking of the cortical surface? Loss of compact bone?

Next, try to categorize the decedent in the photo into one of the categories seen in each of Tables 5.1 through 5.4 (i.e., what stage is it if it were found in a warm, moist climate? In a hot, dry climate? In a cool climate?). Once you have made that determination, enter the appropriate stage and PMI in the surface find section of the Exercise Worksheet 5.1 for each of the three climatic types. If it overlaps with two (or at most three) categories, use the space provided to enter the stage and PMI estimate. Modify your estimate of time since death by taking into account each of the factors queried on the worksheet. How would your estimate change if it were found in water? What if it were buried?

*Table 5.1* Rates of Decomposition in Warm, Moist Climates

| Stage | Decompositional Changes | Time Period |
|---|---|---|
| 1 | Egg masses of insects may be present, appearing like fine sawdust; veins under the skin may be turning blue or dark green; body fluids may be present around nose and mouth. | First Day |
| 2 | Maggots are active on the face; bones around eyes and nose may be exposed; beetles may appear; skin and hair may be slipping from the body; remains emanate odor of decay; abdomen may be bloated; molds begin to appear on the skin; animals may be active; volatile fatty acids may have killed the vegetation immediately around the body. | First week |
| 3 | Maggot activity is less, beetles more common; no bloating; if the body was shaded, bones will be exposed; if the body was not covered, the skin exposed to sunlight will be dry and leathery protecting the maggots from the sun; mammalian carnivores may be removing body parts; molds can be found on the soft tissue as well as on bones; adipocere may be present. | First month |
| 4 | Skeleton is fully exposed and bleached; moss or green algae may be growing on shaded bones; rodent gnawing may be present; animals (e.g., mice, wasps) may nest in the skull. | First year |
| 5 | Exfoliation of cortical bone may be present; longitudinal cracks may occur in long bones exposed to sun; roots of plants may be growing in or through bones; rodent gnawing may be extensive. | First decade |

Summarized from Bass (1997).

*Table 5.2* Stages of Decomposition in Hot, Dry Climates (e.g., Arizona)

| Stage | Label | Description |
|---|---|---|
| 1 | Fresh | Fresh appearance, no discoloration of skin, no insect activity. |
| 2 | Early decomposition | Some flesh relatively fresh; discoloration can vary from gray to green or brown to black; some skin slippage and hair loss; body bloated or deflated; skin may have leathery appearance. |
| 3 | Advanced decomposition | Sagging of flesh; caving of abdominal cavity; loss of internal organs; extensive maggot activity; mummification of outer tissue; less than half of the skeleton exposed; adipocere may be present. |
| 4 | Skeletonization | Decomposing soft tissue with possible desiccation; more than half of the skeleton exposed; some body fluids may be present; greasy to dry bones. |
| 5 | Extreme decomposition | Skeletonization with bleaching and exfoliation; metaphyseal loss; cancellous exposure in vertebrae and long bones. |

Summarized from Table 1 of Galloway et al. (1989).

*Table 5.3* Timetable for Stages of Decomposition in Hot, Arid Climates (e.g., Arizona)

| Stage | Label | Range | Majority (66% or more) |
|---|---|---|---|
| 1 | Fresh | 1 to 7 days | First day |
| 2 | Early decomposition | 1 day to 4 months | 2 to 8 days |
| 3 | Advanced decomposition | 3 days to 3 years | 10 weeks to 4 months |
| 4 | Skeletonization | 7 days to over 3 years | 3 months to 3 years |
| 5 | Extreme decomposition | 2 months to over 3 years | 9 months to over 3 years |

Data compiled from Figure 1 of Galloway et al. (1989).

*Table 5.4* Rates of Decomposition in Cold Climates

| Stage | Label | Description | Range |
|---|---|---|---|
| 1 | Moderate | Partial exposure of bone; loss of body parts; adipocere formation. | 3.5 months or less |
| 2 | Advanced | Loss of internal organs; moderate bone exposure; extensive adipocere. | 1.5 months to 2.7 years |
| 3 | Skeleton, with little soft tissue | Complete exposure of some bony elements; only desiccated soft tissue remaining. | 4 months to 3.5 years |
| 4 | Completely skeletonized | No soft tissue recovered. | 2 months to 8 years |

Compiled from data presented in Komar (1998).

## Exercise 5.2: Estimating PMI Using TADS and ADD

Commence this lab by familiarizing yourself with the concepts of Total Body Score (TBS), Total Aquatic Decomposition Score (TADS), and Accumulated Degree Days (ADD) described in the textbook. Now, examine the photos provided by your instructor and attempt to categorize the amount of decomposition in the face, torso, and limbs. Starting with the face (often a gruesome task), assign the best estimate of Facial Aquatic Decomposition Score (FADS) using Table 5.5 of this manual. Does the face look undamaged (FADS: 1), or is there discoloration with goose pimpling (FADS: 2), or more severe damage (e.g., bone exposed over orbits, frontal, and parietals; FADS: 6). Perform the same process on the torso to determine a Body Aquatic Decomposition Score (BADS) using Table 5.6 of this manual, and on the limbs to determine a Limb Aquatic Decomposition Score (LADS) from Table 5.7. Once you

*Table 5.5* Stages of Decomposition in the Face[1]

| FADS | Description |
|---|---|
| 1 | No visible changes. |
| 2 | Slight pink discoloration, darkened lips, goose pimpling. |
| 3 | Reddening of face and neck, marbling visible on face. Possible early signs of animal activity/predation-concentrated on the ears, nose, and lips. |
| 4 | Bloating of the face, green discoloration, skin beginning to slough off. |
| 5 | Head hair beginning to slough off-mostly at the front. Brain softening and becoming liquefied. Tissue becoming exposed on face and neck. Green/black discoloration. |
| 6 | Bone becoming exposed/concentrated over the orbital, frontal, and parietal regions. Some of the mandible and maxilla. Early adipocere formation. |
| 7 | More extensive skeletonization on the cranium. Disarticulation of the mandible |
| 8 | Complete disarticulation of the skull from torso. Extensive adipocere formation. |

[1]From Table 1 in Heaton et al. (2010).

*Table 5.6* Stages of Decomposition in the Torso[1]

| BADS | Description |
|---|---|
| 1 | No visible changes. |
| 2 | Slight pink discoloration, goose pimpling. |
| 3 | Yellow/green discoloration of abdomen and upper chest. Marbling. Internal organ beginning to decompose/autolysis. |
| 4 | Dark green discoloration of abdomen, mild bloating of abdomen, initial skin slippage. |
| 5 | Green/purple discoloration, extensive abdominal bloating, tense to touch, swollen scrotum in males, exposure of underlying fat and tissues. |
| 6 | Black discoloration, bloating becoming softer, initial exposure of internal organs and bones. |
| 7 | Further loss of tissues and organs, more bone exposed, initial adipocere formation. |
| 8 | Complete skeletonization and disarticulation. |

[1]From Table 2 in Heaton et al. (2010).

*Table 5.7* Stages of Decomposition in the Limbs[1]

| LADS | Description |
|---|---|
| 1 | No visible changes. |
| 2 | Mild wrinkling of skin on hands and/or feet. Possible goose pimpling. |
| 3 | Skin on palms of hands and/or soles of feet becoming white, wrinkled, and thickened. Slight pink discoloration of arms and legs. |
| 4 | Skin on palms of hands and/or soles of feet becoming soggy and loose. Marbling the limbs, predominantly on upper arms and legs. |
| 5 | Skin on hands/feet starting to slough off. Yellow/green to green/black discoloration on arms and/or legs. Initial skin slippage on arms and/or legs. |
| 6 | Degloving of hands and/or feet exposing large areas of underlying muscles and tendons. Patchy sloughing of skin on arms and/or legs. |
| 7 | Exposure of bones of hands and/or feet. Muscles, tendons, and small areas of bone exposed in the lower arms and/or legs. |
| 8 | Bones of hands and/or feet beginning to disarticulate. Bones of upper arms and/or legs becoming exposed. |
| 9 | Complete skeletonization and disarticulation of limbs. |

[1]From Table 3 in Heaton et al. (2010).

*Table 5.8* Total Aquatic Decomposition Score (TADS) and Predicted Accumulative Degree Days (ADD)[1]

| TADS | Predicted ADD | Lower 95% CI | Upper 95% CI |
|---|---|---|---|
| 5 | 13.16 | 3.550 | 45.88 |
| 6 | 17.70 | 4.825 | 61.52 |
| 7 | 23.79 | 6.552 | 82.58 |
| 8 | 31.99 | 8.889 | 110.9 |
| 9 | 43.01 | 12.05 | 149.2 |
| 10 | 57.83 | 16.31 | 200.8 |
| 11 | 77.76 | 22.07 | 270.5 |
| 12 | 104.5 | 29.82 | 364.9 |
| 13 | 140.6 | 40.26 | 492.6 |
| 14 | 189.0 | 54.31 | 665.6 |
| 15 | 254.1 | 73.18 | 900.3 |
| 16 | 341.7 | 98.51 | 1219 |
| 17 | 459.4 | 132.5 | 1652 |
| 18 | 617.7 | 178.0 | 2241 |
| 19 | 830.5 | 238.9 | 3043 |
| 20 | 1117 | 320.4 | 4135 |
| 21 | 1501 | 429.3 | 5625 |
| 22 | 2019 | 574.7 | 7659 |
| 23 | 2714 | 768.6 | 10437 |
| 24 | 3549 | 1027 | 14235 |
| 25 | 4906 | 1371 | 19432 |

[1]From Table 5 in Heaton et al. (2010).

have made these determinations, enter the scores on Exercise Worksheet 5.2 for each of the three anatomical regions (i.e., face, body, limbs), and add them to obtain the sum.

Now, using Table 5.8 of this manual, find the ADD for the TADS calculated above. Enter the Predicted ADD, Upper 95% Limit, and Lower 95% Limit in the spaces provided on Exercise Worksheet 5.2. Notice there are three spaces for each value, corresponding to three average water temperatures (in degrees Celsius). Now divide the ADD values by the degrees and enter the PMI (in days) in the spaces provided. Notice that the PMI for colder water (i.e., 5°) is longer than for the warmer water temperatures (e.g., 10°, 15°) and that there is a considerable range of PMI values for the calculated value of TADS. Write any observations you feel are appropriate in the comments area.

## Exercise 5.3: Estimating PMI Using Animal Scavenging

As described in the textbook, the amount of destruction to bodies caused by animals can be used to estimate time since death. Start this section of the lab by reviewing Table 5.9 in this manual. As can be seen, loss of body segments is a useful indicator of the amount of time a body has been scavenged. Also notice that skeletonization (loss of soft tissue) is another indicator of PMI. Once you learn the individual characteristics, learn their severity within the different stages of scavenging. Now view the time ranges associated with the different stages. Notice the span of time each encompasses and remember that the low end of the range is applicable to cases where factors are optimal (e.g., easy access by many carnivores), while the high end applies to bodies that are harder to access. Finally, review in the textbook data concerning PMI and percentage of the skeleton recovered. If only 20% of a skeleton is recovered at the time of its discovery, then a PMI of 6 months to over 4 years is indicated. Thus, a body represented only by the lower limbs or only by the head and thorax would represent a PMI of this length. However, if 80% or more of the skeleton is recovered, then a time since death of less than 6 months is indicated. This would be indicated if the arms, legs, head, thorax, and vertebral column were mostly present (e.g., only hands and feet are missing, or only one limb is missing).

Now view the photos supplied by your lab instructor. Is the body fresh or is the soft tissue missing? If there are signs of scavenging, is the anterior rib cage (ventral thorax) present or missing? How about the upper extremities? Lower extremities? Does the entire skeleton appear to be disarticulated, except perhaps the vertebral column? Can you determine the amount of the skeleton that is present? Can you see the arms? The legs?

Now complete Exercise Worksheet 5.3 by entering the PMI in the space provided for each case (i.e., photo). If two stages are visible in the case, then the best PMI is from the high end of the lower stage and the low end of the higher stage. Now, try to estimate the amount of the skeleton that is present. Is there 80% or more, or is there less than 20%? Circle the appropriate amount, and enter the PMI in the space provided. Finally, write a justification for your estimates as well as any comments that you feel are needed.

## Exercise 5.4: Estimating PMI Using Deterioration of Clothing and Other Materials

As a last exercise, attempt to determine PMI by viewing the deterioration of paper money and clothing found in association with a body. Familiarize yourself with Table 5.10 in the textbook. Notice that for surface or buried materials, there are three stages of deterioration: mild, severe, and destruction. *Mild* refers to damage that is noticeable, but not worthy of comment; this is similar to that seen in objects that are relatively old, and exhibit only normal "wear and tear." *Severe* indicates evidence of heavy use with holes and tears in the materials. *Destruction* would be evidenced by a shirt in tatters, money that disintegrates when removed from the ground, and other such conditions. Although these are subjective, a little practice will make it easy to recognize each of these stages.

*Table 5.9* Stages of Decomposition From Animal Scavenging

| Stage | Description | Range |
| --- | --- | --- |
| 0 | Early Scavenging of soft tissue<br>No body unit removed | 4 hours to 14 days |
| 1 | Destruction of the ventral thorax<br>Evisceration<br>Removal of one or both upper extremities<br>Removal of scapulae<br>Removal of partial or complete clavicles | 22 days to 2.5 months |
| 2 | Lower extremities fully or partially removed | 2 to 4.5 months |
| 3 | All skeletal elements disarticulated<br>Segments of the vertebral column articulated | 2 to 11 months |
| 4 | Total disarticulation<br>Only cranium recovered<br>Assorted skeletal elements or fragments recovered | 5 to 52 months |

From Haglund (1997).

Now examine the articles provided in the lab. For paper money, determine the stage that best describes its condition. How old is it if it was found on the surface? How old if buried? Now look at the clothing. Determine the material by viewing the label. How old is it if it was found on the surface? If found buried? Using Exercise Worksheet 5.4, estimate the condition of each of the articles given in the lab. Circle the appropriate cell in the table for each article. Now estimate the PMI for each article. Finally, assume that all articles come from the same case and develop a range chart for all articles. What is the best estimate of time since death? Note this on the exercise worksheet and justify your answer.

## NOTE TO INSTRUCTORS

Since most schools will not have fresh forensic cases that students can use to help determine time since death, photos of bodies in various stages of decomposition and animal scavenging for use in your lab will have to be obtained elsewhere. A simple adjunct to this is deteriorated clothing and paper money. These items can be homemade simply by burying or laying paper money ($1 bills) and clothing of different materials in an outdoor location (e.g., your backyard) that is protected from human intrusion. If this is done at the beginning of the semester and exposed to the elements for approximately a month, they should be useful in teaching this lab.

Exercise Worksheets 5.1 and 5.3 from earlier editions have been heavily modified in hopes of making them more useable. In Exercise Worksheet 5.1, there is room for four cases to be assigned a PMI for each of the three climates where schedules exist. In addition, there is room for an estimate of PMI for buried and submerged remains for each climate, but the overall PMI estimate has been removed. Thus, using the **1: Case/Accession number:** section, you can have your students enter the appropriate stage and PMI for each climate for the same photo of a decomposed body, and have them estimate PMI for buried and submerged. You then may want your students to comment on how similar, or dissimilar, the PMI estimates are between the three climates for the same case and give reasons for these findings. Exercise Worksheet 5.3 can be used in a similar manner for PMI from animal scavenging using both stages and percentage of skeleton recovered.

**Exercise Worksheet 5.1: Estimating PMI Using General Decomposition**

Name: _____ Date: _____

**1: Case/Accession number:** _____

Surface Find

Warm, moist climates    Stage: _____    PMI range: _____

Hot, dry climates    Stage: _____    PMI range: _____

Cold climates    Stage: _____    PMI range: _____

Buried Remains                                                                Submerged Remains

Warm, moist climates    PMI range: _____    PMI range: _____

Hot, dry climates    PMI range: _____    PMI range: _____

Cold climates    PMI range: _____    PMI range: _____

Comments: _____
_____
_____

**2: Case/Accession number:** _____

Surface Find

Warm, moist climates    Stage: _____    PMI range: _____

Hot, dry climates    Stage: _____    PMI range: _____

Cold climates    Stage: _____    PMI range: _____

Buried Remains                                                                Submerged Remains

Warm, moist climates    PMI range: _____    PMI range: _____

Hot, dry climates    PMI range: _____    PMI range: _____

Cold climates    PMI range: _____    PMI range: _____

Comments: _____
_____
_____

**3: Case/Accession number:** _____

Surface Find

   Warm, moist climates     Stage: _____     PMI range: _____

   Hot, dry climates     Stage: _____     PMI range: _____

   Cold climates     Stage: _____     PMI range: _____

Buried Remains                                         Submerged Remains

   Warm, moist climates     PMI range: _____     PMI range: _____

   Hot, dry climates     PMI range: _____     PMI range: _____

   Cold climates     PMI range: _____     PMI range: _____

**Comments:** _____

_____

_____

**4: Case/Accession number:** _____

Surface Find

   Warm, moist climates     Stage: _____     PMI range: _____

   Hot, dry climates     Stage: _____     PMI range: _____

   Cold climates     Stage: _____     PMI range: _____

Buried Remains                                         Submerged Remains

   Warm, moist climates     PMI range: _____     PMI range: _____

   Hot, dry climates     PMI range: _____     PMI range: _____

   Cold climates     PMI range: _____     PMI range: _____

**Comments:** _____

_____

_____

**Exercise Worksheet 5.2: Estimating PMI Using TADS and ADD**

Name: _____ Date: _____

1: Case/Accession number: _____

Facial Aquatic Decomposition Score (FADS)     Score: _____

Body Aquatic Decomposition Score (BADS)     Score: _____

Limb Aquatic Decomposition Score (LADS)     Score: _____

Total Aquatic Decomposition Score (TADS)     Sum: _____

**PMI Calculations**

| Temperature | Parameter | ADD | Divisor | PMI (in days) |
|---|---|---|---|---|
| Cold | Lower 95% Limit: | _____ | ÷ 5 | _____ |
| | Predicted ADD: | _____ | ÷ 5 | _____ |
| | Upper 95% Limit: | _____ | ÷ 5 | _____ |
| Warm | Lower 95% Limit: | _____ | ÷ 10 | _____ |
| | Predicted ADD: | _____ | ÷ 10 | _____ |
| | Upper 95% Limit: | _____ | ÷ 10 | _____ |
| Hot | Lower 95% Limit: | _____ | ÷ 15 | _____ |
| | Predicted ADD: | _____ | ÷ 15 | _____ |
| | Upper 95% Limit: | _____ | ÷ 15 | _____ |

Comments: _____

_____

_____

**Exercise Worksheet 5.3: Estimating PMI Using Animal Scavenging**

Name: _____ Date: _____

**1: Case/Accession number:** _____

    Stage: _____   PMI range: _____

    Percentage of skeleton: 80%+          < 20%
                                (< 6 months)   (6+ months)

    PMI: _____

**2: Case/Accession number:** _____

    Stage: _____   PMI range: _____

    Percentage of skeleton: 80%+          < 20%
                                (< 6 months)   (6+ months)
    PMI: _____

**3: Case/Accession number:** _____

    Stage: _____   PMI range: _____

    Percentage of skeleton: 80%+          < 20%
                                (< 6 months)   (6+ months)
    PMI: _____

**4: Case/Accession number:** _____

    Stage: _____   PMI range: _____

    Percentage of skeleton: 80%+          < 20%
                                (< 6 months)   (6+ months)
    PMI: _____

**Comments:** _____

_____

_____

**Exercise Worksheet 5.4: Estimating PMI Using Deterioration of Clothing and Other Materials**

Name: _____ Date: _____

1: Case/Accession number: _____

### Surface Finds

| Material | Stage | | |
|---|---|---|---|
| | *Mild* | *Severe* | *Destruction* |
| Paper money (unprotected) | 0.5 month | Unknown | 10 months |
| Paper money (protected) | 6 months | Unknown | 36 months |
| Cotton | 1–3 months | Unknown | 7 months |
| Acetate | Unknown | Unknown | Unknown |
| Rayon | 2 months | Unknown | 15 months |
| Silk and wool | 10 months | 15 months | 35 months |

Compiled from data in Morse et al. (1983) and Rowe (1997).

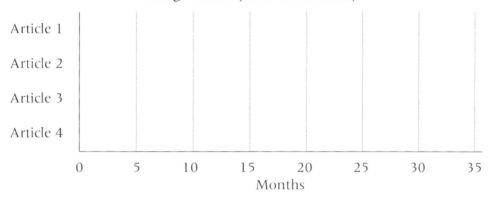

**Range Chart (time in months)**

PMI: _____

Comments: _____
_____

| Buried Finds | | | |
|---|---|---|---|
| Material | Stage | | |
| | *Mild* | *Severe* | *Destruction* |
| Paper money (unprotected) | 0.5 month | 1 month | 2 months |
| Paper money (protected) | 2 months | 6 months | Unknown |
| Cotton | 0.5–10 months | Unknown | 2–10 months |
| Acetate | 2 months | 3–7 months | 8+ months |
| Rayon | 2–7 months | 8–9 months | Unknown |
| Silk and wool | 10 months | 15 months | 35 months |

Compiled from data in Morse et al. (1983) and Rowe (1997).

PMI: _____

**Comments:** _____
_____
_____

# 6  Initial Treatment and Examination

Once human remains have been recovered from the field, four initial steps must be performed before osteological analysis can begin. First, all soft tissue remaining on the bone must be removed so that it does not obscure important features that can help in the identification process. Second, broken bones and structures (e.g., skulls) must be reconstructed, sorted into separate individuals, and reassembled into skeletons in the anatomical position. Third, the individual bones of all represented persons must be inventoried. Last, if the remains are fragmentary and incomplete, an inventory of individual bones and calculation of minimum number of individuals (MNI) must be made. Since most labs do not have the facilities or materials (e.g., cadavers) to teach you how to remove soft tissue, only the reassembling of broken bones, sorting of commingled individuals, and placing skeletons in the anatomical position for inventorying will be done in this lab. Before attempting the exercises given here, familiarize yourself with Chapter 6 in the textbook.

## Learning Objectives

During this lab, you will learn the basics of the initial processes in the analysis of human remains. Specifically, you will learn how to reconstruct broken bones, separate commingled individuals, lay out a skeleton in the anatomical position, and inventory the bones that are present.

## Expected Outcomes

By the end of this lab session, you should be able to:

- Reassemble broken osteological remains.
- Separate commingled individuals.
- Assemble, in the anatomical position, the major elements of the human skeleton (e.g., skull, upper limbs, lower limbs).
- Inventory the bones laid in the anatomical position.

## Minimum Materials

Adult human skeleton (real or plastic, complete or partial)

## Optional Materials

Several adult human skeletons (real or plastic, complete or partial)
Subadult human skeleton (real or plastic, complete or partial)
Broken skeletal remains (needing reconstruction)
Sandbox
Drying racks

## Exercise 6.1: Reconstruction

After the soft tissue has been removed, broken bones must be reconstructed before analysis can continue. Usually, this involves simply gluing together segments to achieve a complete bone. In some cases, reconstruction can be a tedious and difficult task due to the fragmentary nature of the finds; in other cases, only a few broken bones are present. Whether tedious or simple, precision is important, and incorrectly joined fragments should be separated and rejoined to their proper mates. Joining should be done using a glue that is not water soluble (such as Duco® cement), and joined fragments should be placed in specially made sandbox (see Figure 6.3b in the textbook) until they are strong enough to be handled. Improperly glued segments can be separated with acetone before being re-glued to their proper mates. If the bones are unusually fragmented, reinforce the reassembled segments with tape, small wooden sticks (Figure 6.4 in the textbook), or steel rods.

This process is similar to assembling a jigsaw puzzle. Look for segments with similarly shaped edges and check them against each other. To aid you in this, look at the colors of various pieces; in most cases, the pieces of broken bones will be of the same color. For the braincase, it is often helpful to look at the internal features such as the ramifications of the meningeal artery to mate pieces together. For limb bones, look for similarities in curvature of the shafts to help you in reconstruction. No matter what method you use, your best guide is your knowledge of the appearance of complete bones in the human skeleton. There is no worksheet for this exercise.

## Exercise 6.2: Sorting

Sorting commingled skeletons into separate individuals can be started by first separating the bones by type and side. Next, attempt to find the mates of paired bones by knowing that bones from the right side are very close in length and robusticity to their left counterparts. During this process, pay attention to unfused or newly fused epiphyses; if a bone from one side exhibits this, the opposite bone also should show this condition. Now, try articulating bones together to see if they match (see Exercise 6.3 for helpful hints); use Figures 6.6 through 6.15 in the textbook as a guide to show how closely articulated bones should fit. By doing an abbreviated reassembly, separate individuals should emerge.

## Exercise 6.3: Reassembly

Reassembly of a complete or nearly complete skeleton is useful for the further analyses performed in following chapters. Using Figure 6.5 in the textbook, lay the skeleton of each individual in the anatomical position. This involves placing the bones in the same position they are in when persons lie on their backs on a flat surface. The arms are arranged straight along the side with the palms of the hands facing upward and the legs are extended with the feet pointed. In a lab of this type, you may not be able to distinguish left from right, nor separate the hand and foot bones. However, you should be able to determine the superior from the inferior ends of bones so that the major long limb bones are arranged properly. In addition, the photos of bones displayed in the textbook should allow you to properly lay out the pelvic and shoulder areas.

Once this is finished, check the skeleton for the three aspects of internal consistency described in the textbook: duplication, consistency in size, and joint surface concurrence. **Duplication** is easily checked by ensuring that no two bones of the same type and side are present in the skeleton. **Consistency in size** can be checked by ensuring that bones show similar proportions from side to side. The guiding criterion in this analysis is ensuring that a person represented by a skeleton would appear normal. Unless there is a genetic condition present that causes body segments not to be in balance (e.g., certain forms of dwarfism), most people have body portions that "seem right" for their size. Three aspects of bone help determine consistency in size: length, robusticity, and rugosity. Consistency of **length** refers to the similarly proportioned long limb bones, as well as bones of the axial skeleton. Thus, long arms are associated with long legs and torso; also, arms are of such length that the ends of the ulna and radius do not extend farther than the hip socket joint (acetabulum). **Robusticity** means that thick leg bones are not associated with gracile arms; and light bones of the torso are not associated with robust limbs. Lastly, consistency in **rugosity** means that persons with large muscle markings on the arms generally exhibit large muscle markings on the legs.

Finally, use Figures 6.6 through 6.15 in the textbook to ensure **joint surface concurrence,** or that the bone joints appear to fit together; that is, the articular surfaces of the bones should match. Because the body is laid out in the anatomical position, the areas of articulation are in proximity and (at least) extremely dissimilar bones will appear obvious. Starting with the skull, check the jaw with the temporomandibular joints (TMJs). Next, if your lab gets to this level of complexity, check that the atlas articulates with the occipital condyles superiorly and with the axis inferiorly. Again if your lab requires it, continue this process of articulating each vertebra with the one above and below it, down the spinal column to the sacrum and coccyx. Next, ensure that the sacroiliac joints unite to ensure a good fit of the os coxae with the sacrum. Although articulation of the ribs with their respective vertebrae is difficult to accomplish, these bones can be laid out in size order, from smallest to largest going down the body (except for the two floating ribs).

Next, check that the head of the humerus fits against the glenoid cavity of the scapula and that the olecranon process of the ulna articulates with the trochlea of the humerus. Similarly, ensure that the head of the radius fits into the radial notch of the ulna, while the head of the ulna fits into the ulnar notch of the radius. Now, place the head of the femur into the acetabulum and its condyles against the superior end of the tibia. Finally, articulate the fibula with the tibia such that the base of the maleolus of the former fits into the lateral surface on the distal end of the tibia, while the head of the fibula fits against the articular facet of the tibia. Although there is no accompanying worksheet, this exercise is a useful antecedent to the inventory task.

## Exercise 6.4: Inventorying Remains

Once the individuals are sorted, the remains should be inventoried using Exercise Worksheet 6.4. Either adults or subadults (at least 5 years old at the time of death) can be inventoried with these worksheets. Start at the skull and proceed down the axial skeleton and thorax; then move to the appendages, starting first with the upper limbs followed by the bones of the legs. The presence of each bone or epiphysis should be indicated by the percentage of bone present. Simple anthroposcopic estimation is sufficient (e.g., "90% present") with the comments field being used for notes about missing segments. If less precision is desired, you can use "1" for when 75% or more of bone is present, "2" for 25% to 75%, and "3" for less than 25%. Also note the state of preservation of the remains as good (G), fair (F), poor (P), and absent (A); not applicable (N) is used with subadults. In addition, note the color of the bones as well as any weathering; for bones exhibiting cracking and flaking of the cortex, use the categories in Table 6.1 in the textbook. Any inventory or conditions not covered by these categories can be noted in the comments field. Also, if the skeleton is relatively complete (i.e., over 50% of the skeleton is present), blacken the bones that are missing in the skeleton line drawing provided at the end of the worksheets. If the skeletal remains are fragmentary and incomplete (i.e., less than 50% of the skeleton), then blacken the bones that are present.

## Exercise 6.5: Highly Fragmented Remains

As described in the textbook, highly fragmented remains are best analyzed using special Geographic Information System (GIS) software. This software helps to better recognize which osteological elements are present so that a determination of MNI can be made. Since GIS software is too expensive for most schools, in this lab, you will determine MNI using the anthroposcopic methods described in the first paragraph of the Highly Fragmented Remains section of the textbook.

Using Exercise Worksheet 6.5, enter the names of the bone fragments (e.g., proximal humerus, distal tibia) in the left-hand column of the table provided. Now, enter the count of each bone fragment in the next column. If your lab instructor provides information on determining side of a bone, enter the number of left and right fragments in the columns provided. After producing this list, determine the most common fragment by identifying the highest value in the count columns, and enter it in the space provided.

### NOTE TO INSTRUCTORS

Although reconstruction of broken bones may not be feasible in most labs, simple commingling problems, arranging a (full or partial) skeleton in the anatomical position, and inventorying bones can be done even in the most unsophisticated situations. I have used partial plastic skeletons for this exercise and was pleased that students were even able to place long limb bones on their proper sides without being given specific instructions.

You can set up a complex or simple lab as fits your particular style. If you want students to be able to distinguish the bones of the hands and feet, that is certainly possible with the inventory forms presented here. I do not recommend getting to that level but to concentrate only on those bones used in later labs, specifically the skull, long limb bones, and pelvis. Although the worksheets have space for other bones, these labs do not suffer terribly if you ignore the vertebral column, ribs, and hand and foot bones.

**Exercise Worksheet 6.4 A: Inventorying Remains—Adults**

Name: _____    Date: _____

Case number: _____    Individual number: _____

| Cranial Skeleton | | | | |
|---|---|---|---|---|
| *Bone* | *Side* | *Percentage complete* | *Condition (G, F, P, A)* | *Comments (missing elements, color, etc.)* |
| Braincase | | | | |
| Frontal | N/A | | | |
| Parietal | L | | | |
|  | R | | | |
| Temporal | L | | | |
|  | R | | | |
| Occipital | N/A | | | |
| Sphenoid | N/A | | | |
| Face | | | | |
| Nasal | L | | | |
|  | R | | | |
| Maxilla | L | | | |
|  | R | | | |
| Zygomatic | L | | | |
|  | R | | | |
| Lacrymal | L | | | |
|  | R | | | |
| Palatine | L | | | |
|  | R | | | |
| Nasal conchae | L | | | |
|  | R | | | |
| Ethmoid | N/A | | | |
| Vomer | N/A | | | |
| Mandible | N/A | | | |
| Hyoid | | | | |
| Body | N/A | | | |
| Greater cornu | L | | | |
|  | R | | | |

| Appendicular Skeleton | | | | |
|---|---|---|---|---|
| *Bone* | *Side* | *Percentage complete* | *Condition (G, F, P, A)* | *Comments (missing elements, color, etc.)* |
| Upper limbs | | | | |
| Clavicle | L | | | |
| | R | | | |
| Scapula | L | | | |
| | R | | | |
| Humerus | L | | | |
| | R | | | |
| Ulna | L | | | |
| | R | | | |
| Radius | L | | | |
| | R | | | |
| Hands | | | | |
| Carpals | — | — of 16 | | |
| Metacarpals | — | — of 10 | | |
| Phalanges | — | — of 28 | | |
| Lower limbs | | | | |
| Os coxa | L | | | |
| | R | | | |
| Femur | L | | | |
| | R | | | |
| Tibia | L | | | |
| | R | | | |
| Fibula | L | | | |
| | R | | | |
| Patella | L | | | |
| | R | | | |
| Feet | | | | |
| Tarsals | — | — of 14 | | |
| Metatarsals | — | — of 10 | | |
| Phalanges | — | — of 28 | | |

| Axial Skeleton | | | |
|---|---|---|---|
| *Bone* | *Percentage complete* | *Condition (G, F, P, A)* | *Comments (missing elements, color, etc.)* |
| Cervical | | | |
| Atlas | | | |
| Axis | | | |
| C3–C6 | — of 4 | | |
| C7 | | | |
| Thoracic | | | |
| T1–T11 | — of 11 | | |
| T12 | | | |
| Lumbar | | | |
| L1 | | | |
| L2 | | | |
| L3 | | | |
| L4 | | | |
| L5 | | | |
| Sacrum | | | |
| S1 | | | |
| S2 | | | |
| S3 | | | |
| S4 | | | |
| S5 | | | |
| Coccyx | | | |

| Thorax | | | | |
|---|---|---|---|---|
| *Bone* | *Side* | *Percentage complete* | *Condition (G, F, P, A)* | *Comments (missing elements, color, etc.)* |
| Sternum | | | | |
| Manubrium | N/A | | | |
| Body | N/A | | | |
| Xyphoid | N/A | | | |
| Ribs | | | | |
| 1st | L | | | |
| | R | | | |
| 2nd | L | | | |
| | R | | | |
| 3rd–10th | L | — of 8 | | |
| | R | — of 8 | | |
| 11th | L | | | |
| | R | | | |
| 12th | L | | | |
| | R | | | |

**Exercise Worksheet 6.4 B: Inventorying Remains—Subadults**

Name: _____    Date: _____

Case number: _____    Individual number: _____

| Cranial Skeleton | | | | |
|---|---|---|---|---|
| *Bone* | *Side* | *Percentage complete* | *Condition (G, F, P, A)* | *Comments (missing elements, color, etc.)* |
| Braincase | | | | |
| Frontal | N/A | | | |
| Parietal | L | | | |
| | R | | | |
| Temporal | L | | | |
| | R | | | |
| Occipital | N/A | | | |
| Sphenoid | N/A | | | |
| Face | | | | |
| Nasal | L | | | |
| | R | | | |
| Maxilla | L | | | |
| | R | | | |
| Zygomatic | L | | | |
| | R | | | |
| Lacrymal | L | | | |
| | R | | | |
| Palatine | L | | | |
| | R | | | |
| Nasal conchae | L | | | |
| | R | | | |
| Ethmoid | N/A | | | |
| Vomer | N/A | | | |
| Mandible | N/A | | | |
| Hyoid | | | | |
| Body | N/A | | | |
| Greater cornu | L | | | |
| | R | | | |

| Appendicular Skeleton | | | | |
|---|---|---|---|---|
| *Bone* | *Element* | *Condition (G, F, P, A, N)* | | *Comments (missing elements, color, etc.)* |
| | | *Right* | *Left* | |
| Upper limbs | | | | |
| Clavicle | Body | | | |
| | Proximal epiphysis | | | |
| Scapula | Body | | | |
| | Proximal coronoid process | | | |
| | Medical coronoid process | | | |
| | Prox coronoid process | | | |
| | Medical coronoid process | | | |
| | Ventral border | | | |
| | Inferior angle | | | |
| Humerus | Diaphysis | | | |
| | Proximal epiphysis | | | |
| | Distal epiphysis | | | |
| | Medical epicondyle | | | |
| Ulna | Diaphysis | | | |
| | Proximal epiphysis | | | |
| | Distal epiphysis | | | |
| Radius | Diaphysis | | | |
| | Proximal epiphysis | | | |
| | Distal epiphysis | | | |
| Hands | | | | |
| Carpals | Body | — of 16 | | |
| Metacarpals | Body | — of 10 | | |
| | Epiphysis | — of 10 | | |
| Phalanges | Body | — of 28 | | |
| | Epiphysis | — of 28 | | |

| Bone | Element | Condition (G, F, P, A, N) | | Comments (missing elements, color, etc.) |
|------|---------|---------------------------|------|-------------------------------------------|
| | | Right | Left | |
| Lower limbs | | | | |
| Os coxa | Ilium | | | |
| | Ischium | | | |
| | Pubis | | | |
| | Iliac crest | | | |
| | Ischial tuberosity | | | |
| Femur | Diaphysis | | | |
| | Proximal epiphysis | | | |
| | Greater trochanter | | | |
| | Lesser trochanter | | | |
| | Distal epiphysis | | | |
| Tibia | Diaphysis | | | |
| | Proximal epiphysis | | | |
| | Distal epiphysis | | | |
| Fibula | Diaphysis | | | |
| | Proximal epiphysis | | | |
| | Distal epiphysis | | | |
| Patella | Body | | | |
| Feet | | | | |
| Calcaneous | Body | | | |
| | Epiphysis | | | |
| Tarsals | Body | — of 13 | | |
| Metatarsals | Body | — of 10 | | |
| | Epiphysis | — of 10 | | |
| Phalanges | Body | — of 28 | | |
| | Epiphysis | — of 28 | | |

| Axial Skeleton | | | |
|---|---|---|---|
| *Bone* | *Element* | *Condition* <br> *(G, F, P, A, N)* | | *Comments (missing* <br> *elements, color, etc.)* |
| Cervical | | | |
| Atlas | Body | | |
| Axis | Body | | |
| | Dens | — of 4 | | |
| C3–C6 | Body and arch | — of 4 | | |
| | Spinous process | — of 4 | | |
| | Cranial plate | — of 4 | | |
| | Caudal plate | — of 4 | | |
| | Transverse process | — of 4 | — of 4 | |
| C7 | Body and arch | | |
| | Spinous process | | |
| | Cranial plate | | |
| | Caudal plate | | |
| | Transverse process | | |
| Thoracic | | | |
| T1–T11 | Body and arch | — of 11 | | |
| | Spinous process | — of 11 | | |
| | Cranial plate | — of 11 | | |
| | Caudal plate | — of 11 | | |
| | Transverse process | — of 11 | — of 11 | |
| T12 | Body and arch | | |
| | Spinous process | | |
| | Cranial plate | | |

| Bone | Element | Condition (G, F, P, A, N) | Comments (missing elements, color, etc.) |
|---|---|---|---|
|  | Caudal plate |  |  |
|  | Transverse process |  |  |
| Lumbar |  |  |  |
| L1 | Body and arch |  |  |
|  | Spinous process |  |  |
|  | Cranial plate |  |  |
|  | Caudal plate |  |  |
|  | Transverse process |  |  |
| L2 | Body and arch |  |  |
|  | Spinous process |  |  |
|  | Cranial plate |  |  |
|  | Caudal plate |  |  |
|  | Transverse process |  |  |
| L3 | Body and arch |  |  |
|  | Spinous process |  |  |
|  | Cranial plate |  |  |
|  | Caudal plate |  |  |
|  | Transverse process |  |  |
| L4 | Body and arch |  |  |
|  | Spinous process |  |  |
|  | Cranial plate |  |  |
|  | Caudal plate |  |  |
|  | Transverse process |  |  |

| Bone | Element | Condition (G, F, P, A, N) | | Comments (missing elements, color, etc.) |
|---|---|---|---|---|
| L5 | Body and arch | | | |
| | Spinous process | | | |
| | Cranial plate | | | |
| | Caudal plate | | | |
| | Transverse process | | | |
| Sacrum | | | | |
| | Body | — of 5 | | |
| | Cranial plates | — of 5 | | |
| | Caudal plates | — of 5 | | |
| | Arches | — of 5 | — of 5 | |
| | Costal element | — of 3 | — of 3 | |
| | Lateral epiphyses | — of 2 | — of 2 | |
| Coccyx | Segments | — of 4 | | |

| Thorax | | | | |
|---|---|---|---|---|
| Bone | Element | Condition(G, F, P, A, N) | | Comments (missing elements, color, etc.) |
| Sternum | | | | |
| Manubrium | Body | | | |
| Body | — of 4 | | | |
| Xyphoid | Body | | | |
| Ribs | | Right | Left | |
| 1st | Body | | | |
| | Head epiphysis | | | |
| | Articular part of tubercle | | | |

| Bone | Element | Condition(G, F, P, A, N) | | Comments (missing elements, color, etc.) |
|---|---|---|---|---|
|  | Non articular part of tubercle |  |  |  |
| 2nd | Body |  |  |  |
|  | Head epiphysis |  |  |  |
|  | Articular part of tubercle |  |  |  |
|  | Non articular part of tubercle |  |  |  |
| 3rd–10th | Body | — of 8 | — of 8 |  |
|  | Head epiphysis | — of 8 | — of 8 |  |
|  | Articular part of tubercle | — of 8 | — of 8 |  |
|  | Non articular part of tubercle | — of 8 | — of 8 |  |
| 11th | Body |  |  |  |
|  | Head epiphysis |  |  |  |
| 12th | Body |  |  |  |
|  | Head epiphysis |  |  |  |

**Exercise Worksheet 6.5: Highly Fragmented Remains**

Name: _____   Date: _____

Case number: _____

## Cranial Skeleton

| Bone | Total number | Number of left | Number of right | Comments (missing elements, color, etc.) |
|---|---|---|---|---|
| Braincase | | | | |
| Frontal | | N/A | N/A | |
| Parietal | | | | |
| Temporal | | | | |
| Occipital | | N/A | N/A | |
| Sphenoid | | N/A | N/A | |
| Face | | | | |
| Nasal | | | | |
| Maxilla | | | | |
| Zygomatic | | | | |
| Palatine | | | | |
| Mandible | | N/A | N/A | |
| Hyoid | | N/A | N/A | |
| Body | | N/A | N/A | |
| Greater cornu | | | | |

| Appendicular Skeleton | | | | |
|---|---|---|---|---|
| *Bone* | *Total number* | *Number of left* | *Number of right* | *Comments (missing elements, color, etc.)* |
| Upper limbs | | | | |
| Scapula | | | | |
| Humerus | | | | |
| Ulna | | | | |
| Radius | | | | |
| Lower limbs | | | | |
| Os coxa | | | | |
| Femur | | | | |
| Tibia | | | | |

| Axial Skeleton | | |
|---|---|---|
| *Bone* | *Total number* | *Comments (missing elements, color, etc.)* |
| Cervical | | |
| Atlas | | |
| Axis | | |
| Other cervical | | |
| Thoracic | | |
| Lumbar | | |
| Sacrum | | |
| Coccyx | | |

| Thorax | | | | |
|---|---|---|---|---|
| *Bone* | *Total number* | *Number of left* | *Number of right* | *Comments (missing elements, color, etc.)* |
| Sternum | | | | |
| Manubrium | | N/A | N/A | |
| Body | | N/A | N/A | |
| Ribs | | | | |
| 1st | | | | |
| 2nd | | | | |
| 3rd–10th | | | | |
| Floating ribs | | | | |

**Minimum number of individuals:** _____

**Comments:** _____

_____

_____

# 7 Attribution of Ancestry

When in its infancy, the major function provided by forensic anthropology to law enforcement was the identification of demographic characteristics from skeletonized remains. Although the discipline has expanded into areas such as body recovery and trauma analysis, the attribution of ancestry, sex, age, and stature is still the major role of this discipline. This chapter deals with the techniques by which forensic anthropologists attempt to discern the genetic background of individuals represented by their skeletons. As stated in the textbook, this is one of the most difficult assessments from the skeleton. Often, remains exhibit characteristics that can be attributed to two groups. In these cases, ancestry should be assigned to the group that is considered the minority as this is how the person would be perceived in life. Thus, if a skeleton exhibits part White and part Black features, it should be considered Black. Ancestry is attributable only to adults, as a majority of characteristics that help assess this trait are only found in adult remains.

This chapter covers the two basic methods used by forensic anthropologists in ancestral attribution: anthroposcopy and osteometry. Exercises 7.1 and 7.2 deal with the anthroposcopic attribution of ancestry from the human skull. Exercises 7.3 and 7.4 deal with metric methods for assessing ancestry, also from the skull, while Exercise 7.5 uses both anthroposcopic and osteometric methods for determining ancestry from the femur.

## Learning Objectives

During this lab, you will learn the structures of the human skull and femur that can be used to attribute a skeleton to one of three basic ancestral groups common in the United States: White, Black, or Asian. In addition, you will learn the measurements of these two osteological structures that can be used to attribute ancestry.

## Expected Outcomes

By the end of this lab session, you should be able to:

- Attribute ancestral group to a skull by observing its characteristics.
- Attribute ancestral group to a skull from its measurements.
- Attribute ancestry from observations and measurements of the femur.

## Minimum Materials

Human skulls (preferably one from each of the three ancestral groups)

## Optional Materials

Sliding caliper
Spreading caliper
Simometer
Femora (at least one White and one Black)
X-ray machine

## Exercise 7.1: Attributing Ancestry Using Cranial Anthroposcopy

Before commencing, familiarize yourself with the methods used to attribute ancestry to the human skull by reading the description in the Anthroposcopic Traits section of the textbook and viewing the figures within those pages. Next, identify the structures of the nose useful for attributing ancestry: root, bridge, and spine (see Figure 7.1 in this manual). As described in the textbook, the nasal root is the area where the nasal bones articulate with the frontal; the bridge is formed by the nasal bones themselves, and the nasal spine is the projection of bone (if present) forward from the base of the nasal aperture.

After you have familiarized yourself with this material, observe the characteristics in your laboratory skull. Do the nasal root and bridge project forward from the face (as in Figure 7.3a in the textbook), or are they relatively flat and nonprojecting (especially as in Figure 7.3c in the textbook)? Also, observe the maxillae where they merge with the floor of the nose. Is it raised into a sharp "sill" (Figure 7.5a in the textbook), or is it flat or guttered (Figure 7.5b)? Next, observe the shape of the nasal opening; see if it is wide in comparison to its height (e.g., the height and width are approximately the same size) as in Figure 7.4c in the textbook, or narrow (i.e., the width is smaller than the height) as in Figure 7.4a, or intermediate as in Figure 7.4b.

Next, observe the face while holding the side of the skull toward you. Do the jaws project forward (see Figures 7.3b and 7.3c in the textbook), or do they seem to be located more under the eye orbits (Figure 7.3a)? To best observe this characteristic, hold the skull in the Frankfort horizon; that is, hold the skull such that the lower border of the eye is at the same level as the upper border of the ear. Also, does the lower border of the eye project forward of the upper border as in Figure 7.7a in the textbook, or does it fall at the same level (Figure 7.7b) or behind this structure? Now turn the skull to face you and observe the shape of the face; is it approximately as wide as it is high (see facial views in Figures 7.1b and 7.1c in the textbook), or is the width smaller than the height, making the face appear narrow (Figure 7.1a)? Also observe the shape of the eye orbits; are they angular (see Figure 7.2a in this manual), rectangular (with the long dimension being horizontal; see Figure 7.2b in this manual), or are they rounded (Figure 7.2c in this manual)?

Next, observe the vault. Are the browridges large and projecting or small? (This also is a sexual characteristic.) Are the muscle markings rugged and easily visible, or are they relatively smooth and hard to distinguish from the rest of the bone? Is there a depression behind bregma when the skull is observed from the side, or is the area flat or even slightly raised? Are the coronal, sagittal, and lambdoid sutures relatively straight (see Figure 7.3a in this manual), or do they wander from side to side significantly (Figure 7.3b in this manual)?

Lastly, observe the jaws and teeth. Are they large by comparison to the rest of the skull (or other skulls in the lab), or are they relatively small? Does the maxilla project forward such that a line drawn from the tip of the nasals to the most forward point on the maxilla slant backward (as in line 3 in Figure 7.3a in the textbook), or forward (as in line 3

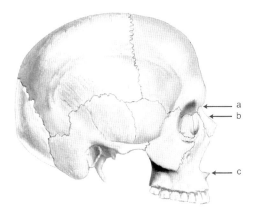

*Figure 7.1* Side view of human nose showing three of five features useful in assessing ancestry: (**a**) root; (**b**) bridge; (**c**) spine.

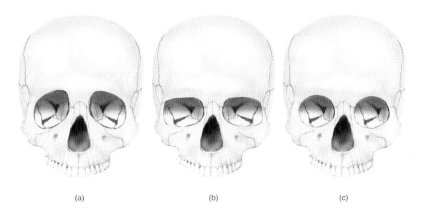

*Figure 7.2* Characteristic shapes of the eye orbits of the three ancestral groups: (**a**) Whites; (**b**) Blacks; (**c**) Asians.

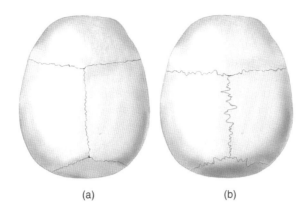

(a)                    (b)

*Figure 7.3* Variations in the complexity of cranial vault sutures: (a) simple in Whites; (b) complex in Asians.

in Figures 7.3b and 7.3c)? Also, turn the skull on its top and view the shape of the dental arch. Is it parabolic, rounded (i.e., curved such that it forms a half circle), or U-shaped (i.e., the sides and the anterior part are each approximately straight and meet at right angles)? Use Figure 7.9 in the textbook to help you in this observation. Finally, looking at the teeth, observe the lingual side of the upper (especially central) incisors; are they flat like a spatula (see Figure 7.10a in the textbook), or are there ridges running along the vertical edges making the surface appear as a shovel (Figure 7.10b)? Also, is there a cusp 7 on the lower first molars (see Figure 7.11a of the textbook) or a Bushman canine (Figure 7.11b of the textbook)?

Now, use the table in Exercise Worksheet 7.1 as a decision matrix (see Chapter 1 of the textbook for a description) to determine which is the likely ancestral group of the skull given to you for analysis. For each characteristic, circle the word in the column that best fits the laboratory skull. (If both columns contain the same word, circle both.) Once completed, count all of the circles in each column and enter the value on the total line. Viewing the totals, write which group the skull is most likely to be from in the space provided; and, enter your justification for making that determination in the comments area. (This is particularly important if characteristics indicate mixed ancestry, or if there are oddities that make the attribution less certain.)

## Exercise 7.2: Attributing Ancestry Using Frequencies of Cranial Anthroposcopic Traits

As described in the textbook, research on ancestry has progressed in recent years. Several of the nasal traits described above have been combined into two (inferior nasal aperture morphology, and nasal bone contour), and the number of categories for these have been increased from three to five. Also, several new traits have been added; these are interobital breadth, nasal overgrowth, and zygomaticomaxillary suture. Most importantly, the frequencies of these characteristics within the three main ancestral groups, as well as Hispanics, have been calculated on different samples. This research is summarized in Figures 7.12 to 7.19 and Table 7.3 of the textbook.

After familiarizing yourself with that information, determine the expression of each trait on the lab specimen. Using the table in Exercise Worksheet 7.2 as a decision matrix, circle the number in all columns that correspond to the expression. For example, if there is a postbregmatic depression, circle the 0.260 for White, 0.466 for Black, 0.080 for Asian, and 0.194 for Hispanic. When finished, add the numbers in the circles by column, and enter the sum in the second to the bottom row of the table. The column with the highest sum is the most likely ancestral group of the lab specimen. If a probability is preferred (i.e., a number between 0 and 1), divide that sum by the number of circles in each column and place the result in the last line of the table. Again, the column with the highest value (i.e., probability) is the most likely ancestral group.

### Exercise 7.3: Attributing Ancestry Using Cranial Metrics: Interorbital Indexes

If your lab has a simometer (see Figure 7.24 in the textbook), perform the measurements necessary to separate Whites from Blacks and Asians using the three interorbital indexes of the midface. Refer to Figure 7.4 in this manual for illustrations of the six measurements and Table 7.1 for definitions of these measurements. Each index consists of a breadth/cord measurement and a subtense (i.e., a projection forward from the line formed by the breadth measurement). Place the tips of the simometer on the landmarks that define the breadth/cord measurement; when they are secured against these points, move the center piece down until it contacts the deepest point on the nasal bones.

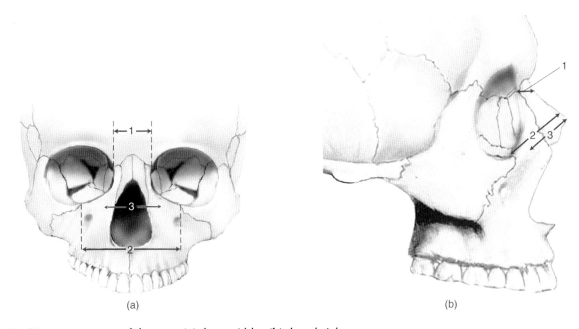

(a)                                                      (b)

*Figure 7.4*  Six measurements of the nose: (**a**) three widths; (**b**) three heights.

*Table 7.1*  Description of Measurements Used in the Interorbital Indexes

| Distance | Term | Description |
|---|---|---|
| *Figure 7.4(a)—Breadths* | | |
| 1 | Maxillofrontal | Straight distance between the maxillofrontal; place the tips of the simometer at the confluence of the frontomaxillary suture with the lacrymal crest. |
| 2 | Midorbital | Straight distance between the zygoorbitale; place the tips of the simometer at the place where the zygomaxillary suture meets the lower border of the eye. |
| 3 | Alpha cord | Straight distance between the points where the nose begins to rise out of the maxilla along the line connecting the two zygoorbitale. |
| *Figure 7.4(b)—Subtenses* | | |
| 1 | Naso–maxillofrontal | Projection from the maxillofrontal breadth to the least projecting point on the nasal bridge; use the center probe of the simometer. |
| 2 | Naso–zygoorbital | Projection from the midorbital breadth to the least projecting point on the nasal bridge; use the center probe of the simometer. |
| 3 | Naso–alpha | Projection from the alpha cord to the least projecting point on the nasal bridge; use the center probe of the simometer. |

After Gill and Gilbert (1990).

Once each measurement is taken, enter the subtense values on the first line of the index equations on Exercise Worksheet 7.2 and the breadth/cord measurements on the second line of each index. Now divide the breadth/cord into the subtense quantity and multiply by 100 to get the index value. Compare that value with the sectioning point given for each formula and circle the appropriate ancestral group(s) for that index (e.g., White or Black/Asian).

### Exercise 7.4: Attributing Ancestry Using Cranial Metrics: Discriminant Functions

Discriminant functions can be used to separate the three ancestral groups using measurements of the skull. Consult Figures 7.5 and 7.6 in this manual for the endpoints of these measurements and Table 7.2 for descriptions of these measurements. Also, it is useful to review the cranial landmarks presented in Chapter 2 in this manual. Use an appropriate

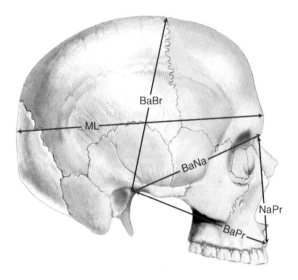

*Figure 7.5* Measurements used in the calculation of discriminant functions (lateral view).

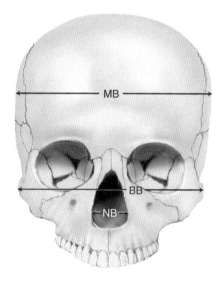

*Figure 7.6* Measurements used in the calculation of discriminant functions (anterior view).

*Table 7.2*  Descriptions of Measurements for Discriminant Functions

| Measurement | Description |
| --- | --- |
| BaPr | Basion to prosthion; use a spreading caliper (although a sliding caliper serves on some skulls); cradle the skull on its side in your lap, place one tip on basion and the other on prosthion. |
| ML | Maximum length; use a spreading or sliding caliper; place the skull on a flat surface with its side toward you; place one tip on glabella and the other on the occipital bone; move the posterior tip up and down while holding the anterior one on glabella until the caliper reads the greatest distance. |
| MB | Maximum breadth; use a spreading or sliding caliper; place the skull on a flat surface facing you; open the calipers and place the tips on the highest point of the squamosal suture; move the tips up and down as well as forward and backward until the caliper reads the greatest distance. |
| BaBr | Basion to bregma; use a spreading or sliding caliper; cradle the skull on its side in your lap; place one tip on basion and the other on Bregma. |
| BaNa | Basion to nasion; use a spreading or sliding caliper; cradle the skull on its side in your lap; place one tip on basion and the other on nasion. |
| BB | Bizygomatic breadth; use a spreading or sliding caliper; cradle the skull on its top in your lap; move the tips of the calipers back and forth along the zygomatic arches while keeping the instrument perpendicular to the sagittal plane. |
| PrNa | Prosthion to nasion; use a spreading or sliding caliper; cradle the skull on its side in your lap; place one tip on prosthion and the other on nasion. |
| NB | Nasal breadth; use a sliding caliper with opposing tips (see Figure 1.8a of the textbook); cradle the skull on its back in your lap; place the tips inside the nose and find the widest distance. |

*Table 7.3* Discriminant Functions for Distinguishing Whites, Blacks, and Native Americans

| Cranial Measurement | Males Whites Versus | | Females Whites Versus | |
|---|---|---|---|---|
| | Blacks | Native Americans | Blacks | Native Americans |
| Basion to prosthion (BaPr) | 3.06 | 0.10 | 1.74 | 3.05 |
| Maximum length (ML) | 1.60 | −0.25 | 1.28 | −1.04 |
| Maximum breadth (MB) | −1.90 | −1.56 | −1.18 | −5.41 |
| Basion to bregma (BaBr) | −1.79 | 0.73 | −0.14 | 4.29 |
| Basion to nasion (BaNa) | −4.41 | −0.29 | −2.34 | −4.02 |
| Bizygomatic breadth (BB) | −0.10 | 1.75 | 0.38 | 5.62 |
| Prosthion to nasion (PrNa) | 2.59 | −0.16 | −0.01 | −1.00 |
| Nasal breadth (NB) | 10.56 | −0.88 | 2.45 | −2.19 |
| Sectioning points | 89.27 | 22.28 | 92.20 | 130.10 |

measuring instrument (i.e., spreading or sliding calipers); place its tips on the landmarks that define the measurement and read the value from the caliper scale. As the measurements are taken, enter their values in the appropriate columns of the Exercise Worksheet 7.3. Ask the instructor for the sex of the assigned skull (you will learn how to attribute sex in the next chapter); use Exercise Worksheet 7.3 A for males and Exercise Worksheet 7.3 B for females.

After calculating the function values for White versus Black and White versus Native American, circle the appropriate ancestral group by comparing the function value with sectioning points given on the exercise sheets.

Now go to the last table on the exercise sheet and circle the appropriate row in the Function Results column (e.g., if the results of both discriminant functions indicate White, then circle the White–White row) and read the ancestry of the individual from the Ancestral Group column. If the discriminant function results indicate Black–Native American, an extra step must be performed. If the individual being studied is male, enter the total from the White–Black function in the space provided (W–B Total). Now, place the total from the White–Native American function on the space provided (W–NA Total), multiply it by the coefficient (i.e., 3.99) and place the result on the preceding line. Compare the two values; if the W–B Total is greater than the result of the multiplication by 3.99, then the individual is Black (circle the ">" sign); if the W–B Total is less than the W–NA calculation, then the individual is Native American (circle the "<" sign). The same process applies if the individual being studied is female, except the White–Native American function total is multiplied by 0.709 (instead of 3.99).

## Exercise 7.5: Attributing Ancestry Using Postcranial Anthroposcopy and Osteometry

As mentioned in Chapter 7 in the textbook, there are several methods for attributing ancestry from the postcranial skeleton. However, this exercise will only deal with the femur. Take the laboratory bone and hold it upright with the medial or lateral side toward you. Does the shaft bend in the middle anteriorly, or is it relatively straight from the superior to inferior ends? To help you in this determination, consult Figure 7.7 in this manual. Next, check the torsion of the head and neck by laying the bone on a flat surface (e.g., lab table) with the posterior side down and both condyles contacting the surface (see Figure 7.8 in this manual). Does the head and neck of the femur lie almost parallel with the flat surface, or do they angle upward? If the bone has a straight shaft and a head and neck close to the surface, it is probably Black; however, if the shaft is curved and the head and neck are not angled upward, it is probably White. Asian ancestry (including Native American) is indicated by a curved shaft and angled head and neck. Now measure the anterior–posterior (A–P) and medial–lateral (M–L) widths of the femur immediately distal to the lesser trochanter. Enter the measurements into the following formula for the Platymeric Index (PI):

$$PI = \frac{(A-P)}{(M-L)} \times 100$$

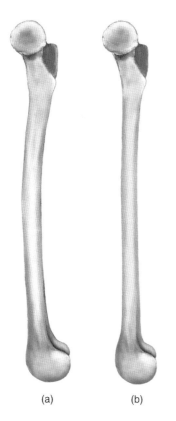

*Figure 7.7* Profile of the femur showing: (**a**) curved of Asians and Whites; (**b**) straight of Blacks.

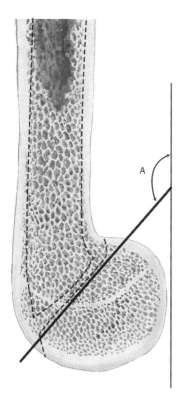

*Figure 7.9* The intercondylar shelf and its attendant angle for attributing ancestry.

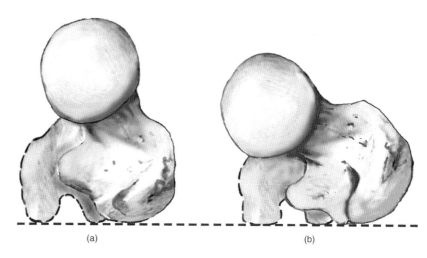

*Figure 7.8* Torsion of the femoral neck: (**a**) strong torsion typical of Native Americans; (**b**) mild torsion typical of Whites and Blacks.

Reprinted from Figure 2 by TD Stewart (1962) *Human Biology: The International Journal of Population Genetics and Anthropology*, Vol 34:49–62. Copyright © Wayne State University Press, with the permission of Wayne State University Press.

If the value is below 84.3, the specimen is likely to be Native American. However, if it is above that value, ancestry cannot be told. Finally, if an X-ray machine is available, make a radiograph of the distal femur. Using a grease pencil, draw a line adjacent to the posterior surface of the condyles that is parallel to the long axis of the bone and another line parallel to the intercondylar shelf (see Figure 7.9 in this manual). Now measure angle *A*. If that angle is higher than 141°, the femur is more likely White; if less than that value, it is more likely Black. Enter all of your findings on Exercise Worksheet 7.4 and make a best estimate of ancestry based on your observations and measurements.

## NOTE TO INSTRUCTORS

It would be difficult to offer this lab without skulls of at least two of the three ancestral groups. Casts of these can be obtained from the sources described in the Sources of Materials section. (Unfortunately, the Carolina Biological Supply plastic skulls are no longer available.) Also, interesting labs can result when a subgroup of students does Exercise Worksheets 7.1., 7.2, 7.3 (if a sinometer is available), and 7.4 on a single skull.

**Exercise Worksheet 7.1: Attributing Ancestry Using Cranial Anthroposcopy**

Name: _____     Date: _____

Case/Accession number: _____

| Structure | Whites | Blacks | Asians |
|---|---|---|---|
| Nose | | | |
| Root | High, narrow | Low, rounded | Low, ridged |
| Bridge | High | Low | Low |
| Spine | Pronounced | Small | Small |
| Lower border | Sharp (sill) | Guttered | Flat, sharp |
| Width | Narrow | Wide | Medium |
| Face | | | |
| Profile | Straight | Projecting | Intermediate |
| Shape | Narrow | Narrow | Wide |
| Eye orbits | Angular | Rectangular | Rounded |
| Lower eye border | Receding | Receding | Projecting |
| Vault | | | |
| Browridges | Heavy | Small | Small |
| Muscle marks | Rugged | Smooth | Smooth |
| Vault sutures | Simple | Simple | Complex |
| Post-bregma | Straight | Depressed | Straight |
| Jaws and Teeth | | | |
| Jaws | Small | Large | Medium |
| Palatal shape | Parabolic | Hyperbolic | Elliptical |
| Upper incisors | Spatulate | Spatulate | Shoveled |
| Cusp-7 | Absent | Present | Absent |
| Bushman canine | Absent | Present | Absent |
| **Total count** | _____ | _____ | _____ |

Compiled from information in Brues (1977), Krogman (1962), and Rhine (1990).

**Ancestral group:** _____

**Comments:** _____

_____

_____

**Exercise Worksheet 7.2: Attributing Ancestry Using Frequencies of Cranial Anthroposcopic Traits**

Name: _____     Date: _____

Case/Accession number: _____

| Trait | Category | White | Black | Asian | Hispanic |
|---|---|---|---|---|---|
| Anterior Nasal Spine (Figure 7.12) | 1 | 0.144 | 0.288 | 0.486 | 0.082 |
| | 2 | 0.243 | 0.241 | 0.112 | 0.404 |
| | 3 | 0.435 | 0.204 | 0.094 | 0.267 |
| Inferior Nasal Aperture Morphology (Figure 7.13) | 1 | 0.044 | 0.687 | 0.269 | 0.000 |
| | 2 | 0.076 | 0.480 | 0.350 | 0.093 |
| | 3 | 0.195 | 0.237 | 0.460 | 0.108 |
| | 4 | 0.383 | 0.124 | 0.081 | 0.413 |
| | 5 | 0.376 | 0.094 | 0.024 | 0.506 |
| Interorbital Breadth (Figure 7.14) | 1 | 0.277 | 0.094 | 0.372 | 0.257 |
| | 2 | 0.269 | 0.184 | 0.259 | 0.288 |
| | 3 | 0.144 | 0.655 | 0.068 | 0.132 |
| Nasal Aperture Width (Figure 7.15) | 1 | 0.586 | 0.041 | 0.080 | 0.292 |
| | 2 | 0.190 | 0.191 | 0.340 | 0.279 |
| | 3 | 0.152 | 0.572 | 0.137 | 0.139 |
| Nasal Bone Contour (Figure 7.16) | 0 | 0.073 | 0.521 | 0.319 | 0.087 |
| | 1 | 0.169 | 0.237 | 0.282 | 0.312 |
| | 2 | 0.179 | 0.155 | 0.615 | 0.050 |
| | 3 | 0.298 | 0.143 | 0.178 | 0.381 |
| | 4 | 0.446 | 0.307 | 0.034 | 0.213 |
| Nasal Overgrowth (Figure 7.17) | 0 | 0.251 | 0.316 | 0.269 | 0.164 |
| | 1 | 0.253 | 0.177 | 0.228 | 0.342 |
| Postbregmatic Depression (Figure 7.18) | 0 | 0.247 | 0.173 | 0.311 | 0.269 |
| | 1 | 0.260 | 0.466 | 0.080 | 0.194 |

| Zygomaticomaxillary Suture (Figure 7.19) | 0 | 0.137 | 0.144 | 0.059 | 0.660 |
| | 1 | 0.259 | 0.268 | 0.236 | 0.236 |
| | 2 | 0.297 | 0.284 | 0.356 | 0.063 |

Sum

Probability

1  Combined from information in Hefner (2009), Hefner et al. (2015), and Klales and Kenyhercz (2015). All figure numbers from textbook.

**Ancestral group:** _____

**Comments:** _____

_____

_____

**Exercise Worksheet 7.3: Attributing Ancestry Using Cranial Metrics: Interorbital Indexes**

Name: _____ Date: _____

Case/Accession number: _____

## Maxillofrontal Index

Naso–maxillo
frontal subtense _____ ÷ _____ Maxillofrontal
breadth × 100 = _____ Maxillofrontal
index

(Black/Asian < 40 < White)

## Zygoorbital Index

Naso–zygoorbital
subtense _____ ÷ _____ Midorbital
breadth × 100 = _____ Zygoorbital
index

(Black/Asian < 38 < White)

## Alpha Index

(Sectioning point: If greater than 60, then White)

Naso–alpha
subtense _____ ÷ _____ Alpha cord × 100 = _____ Alpha index

(Black/Asian < 60 < White)

**Ancestral group:** _____

**Comments:** _____

_____

_____

## Exercise Worksheet 7.4 A: Attributing Ancestry Using Cranial Metrics: Discriminant Functions (Males)

Name: _____ Date: _____

Case/Accession number: _____

### Whites Versus Blacks

| Measurement | Value | | Coefficient | | Calculation |
|---|---|---|---|---|---|
| BaPr | _____ | × | 3.06 | = | _____ |
| ML | _____ | × | 1.60 | = | _____ |
| MB | _____ | × | −1.90 | = | _____ |
| BaBr | _____ | × | −1.79 | = | _____ |
| BaNa | _____ | × | −4.41 | = | _____ |
| BB | _____ | × | −0.10 | = | _____ |
| PrNa | _____ | × | 2.59 | = | _____ |
| NB | _____ | × | 10.56 | = | _____ |
| Total | | | | | |

Sectioning point (circle one):                                              White < 62.89 < Black

After Table 26 and page 121 of Ubelaker (1999). Courtesy of Taraxacum Press.

### Whites Versus Native Americans

| Measurement | Value | | Coefficient | | Calculation |
|---|---|---|---|---|---|
| BaPr | _____ | × | 0.10 | = | _____ |
| ML | _____ | × | −0.25 | = | _____ |
| MB | _____ | × | −1.56 | = | _____ |
| BaBr | _____ | × | 0.73 | = | _____ |
| BaNa | _____ | × | −0.29 | = | _____ |
| BB | _____ | × | 1.75 | = | _____ |
| PrNa | _____ | × | −0.16 | = | _____ |
| NB | _____ | × | −0.88 | = | _____ |
| Total | | | | | _____ |

Sectioning point (circle one):                                              White < 22.28 < Asian

| Function Results | Ancestral Group | | | | |
|---|---|---|---|---|---|
| White–White | White | | | | |
| White–Native American | Native American | | | | |
| Black–White | Black | | | | |
| Black–Native American | _____ | < | > | _____ = 3.99* _____ | |
| | W–B Total | Native American | Black | W–NA Total | |

**Comments:** _____

_____

_____

_____

**Exercise Worksheet 7.4 B: Attributing Ancestry Using Cranial Metrics: Discriminant Functions (Females)**

Name: _____  Date: _____

Case/Accession number: _____

## Whites Versus Black

| Measurement | Value | | Coefficient | | Calculation |
|---|---|---|---|---|---|
| BaPr | _____ | × | 1.74 | = | _____ |
| ML | _____ | × | 1.28 | = | _____ |
| MB | _____ | × | −1.18 | = | _____ |
| BaBr | _____ | × | −0.14 | = | _____ |
| BaNa | _____ | × | −2.34 | = | _____ |
| BB | _____ | × | 0.38 | = | _____ |
| PrNa | _____ | × | −0.01 | = | _____ |
| NB | _____ | × | 2.45 | = | _____ |
| Total | | | | | _____ |

Sectioning point (circle one):                    White < 92.20 < Black

## Whites Versus Native American

| Measurement | Value | | Coefficient | | Calculation |
|---|---|---|---|---|---|
| BaPr | _____ | × | 3.05 | = | _____ |
| ML | _____ | × | −1.04 | = | _____ |
| MB | _____ | × | −5.41 | = | _____ |
| BaBr | _____ | × | 4.29 | = | _____ |
| BaNa | _____ | × | −4.02 | = | _____ |
| BB | _____ | × | 5.62 | = | _____ |
| PrNa | _____ | × | −1.00 | = | _____ |
| NB | _____ | × | −2.19 | = | _____ |
| Total | | | | | |

**Sectioning point (circle one):**                     White < 130.10 < Asian

| Function Results | Ancestral Group | | | |
|---|---|---|---|---|
| White–White | White | | | |
| White–Native American | Native American | | | |
| Black–White | Black | | | |
| Black–Native American | _____ | < | > | _____ = 0.709* _____ |
| | W–B Total | Native American | Black | W–NA Total |

Comments: _____

_____

_____

_____

**Exercise Worksheet 7.5: Attributing Ancestry Using Postcranial Anthroposcopy and Osteometry**

Name: _____     Date: _____

Case/Accession number: _____

Platymeric Index = _____ × 100 = _____

| Characteristic | Ancestral Group | | |
| --- | --- | --- | --- |
| | *White* | *Blacks* | *Asian* |
| Shaft | Curved | Straight | Curved |
| Torsion | Mild | Mild | Severe |
| PI < 84.3 | No | No | Yes |
| Intercondylar shelf angle | > 141° | < 142° | N/A |
| Total count | _____ | _____ | _____ |

Ancestral group: _____

Comments: _____

_____

_____

# 8 Attribution of Sex

As described in the textbook, the attribution of sex is another key demographic characteristic needed by law enforcement officials to search their missing persons files. Although sexing can be done with the full skeleton, individual bones and structures (e.g., the pelvis, the skull) also yield information on this trait. In this lab, you will look at each structure or bone and then attribute sex based on the central tendency of the data. Remember, the most accurate assessment of sex can be derived from the complete skeleton, followed in accuracy by the pelvis, skull, and then individual postcranial bones. This should be kept in mind when doing the exercises presented in this chapter.

## Learning Objectives

In this lab, you will learn those features of the skeleton that can be used to attribute sex. You will also learn the measurements and observations of the pelvis, skull, and postcranial bones that will help you in this endeavor.

## Expected Outcomes

By the end of this lab session, you should be able to:

- Distinguish male from female skeletons from observations of the pelvis.
- Distinguish male from female skeletons from measurements of the pelvis.
- Distinguish male from female skeletons from observations of the skull.
- Distinguish male from female skeletons from measurements of the skull.
- Distinguish male from female from measurements of single bones of the skeleton.

## Minimum Materials

Pelvises—one male, one female
Skulls—one male, one female

## Optional Materials

Scapula
Humerus
Radius
Femur

## Exercise 8.1: Attributing Sex Using Pelvic Anthroposcopy

Before beginning to identify sexual characteristics, review the anatomy of the pelvis in Chapter 2 of the textbook and Figures 2.27 through 2.31. The pelvis is composed of three bones: right and left os coxa and the sacrum; identify these bones in the laboratory pelvis. In addition, identify the three bones of the os coxa: ilium, ischium, and pubis; use Figure 8.8 in the textbook to help you distinguish where the ilium and pubis join superiorly. Also, notice where the ischim and pubis join inferiorly; this usually can be seen as a roughened area located toward the center of the bottom margin of the os coxa. In addition to Chapter 2, read the section "Sexing the Pelvis" in Chapter 8 of the textbook.

Now, view the laboratory pelvis. Is it larger and more rugged than other pelvises in the laboratory? Is it tall and narrow or short and wide as illustrated in Figure 8.1 of the textbook? In addition, is the pelvic inlet (the area enclosed by the os coxae and sacrum when viewed superiorly) heart-shaped or more oval (see Figure 8.2 in the textbook)?

Next, look at features of individual bones to help determine sex. Is the shape of the pubis rectangular or square (see Figure 8.5a in the textbook)? Does the bone appear stretched (Figure 8.5b, *right*)? Now look at the subpubic angle (see Figure 8.1 in the textbook). Is it V-shaped and less than 90° (Figure 8.1b in this manual), or more rounded (or U-shaped) with an angle over 90° (Figure 8.1a)? To measure the angle of an articulated pelvis, lay it down with the pubic bones against a piece of paper and trace the outline of the subpubic angle (see Figure 8.1 of this manual). Now, draw straight lines adjacent to that part of the trace from the place of meeting of the pubic bones until the trace lines begin to curve. Use a protractor to measure the angle formed by these lines.

Next, observe the obturator foramen. Is it an oval or a triangle? Look at the greater sciatic notch. Is it wide and spacious (Figure 8.3a in the textbook), or narrow and constricted (Figure 8.3b)? Also, compare it with the different grades of this structure presented in Figure 8.2 of this manual; try to determine which of these best illustrates the lab pelvis. Similarly, is the preauricular sulcus wide and well-developed (arrows in Figure 8.3a in the textbook) or narrow (or even absent)? Finally, using Figure 8.4 of the textbook as a reference, look at the sacrum; is it long and narrow with an even anterior–posterior curvature, or wide and short with a marked anterior angulation of segments 3 through 5?

Now, use the table in Exercise Worksheet 8.1 as a decision matrix (see Chapter 1 of the textbook for a description) to determine which is the likely sex of the lab pelvis. For each characteristic, circle the expression that best fits the laboratory pelvis. Once completed, count the number of circles in each column, and enter the value on the total line. Now, viewing the totals, write the most likely sex of the pelvis in the space provided.

In addition to these classic traits of the entire pelvis, three other characteristics, described by Phenice (1969), aid in sexing the pelvis. These are presented in Table 8.2 of the textbook, and the first two are illustrated in Figure 8.5 of the textbook. Find the ventral arc (if present) on your laboratory pelvis. Figure 8.5a illustrates the manifestation of this

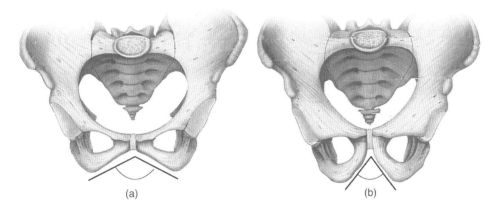

*Figure 8.1* Measurement of the subpubic angle to attribute sex.

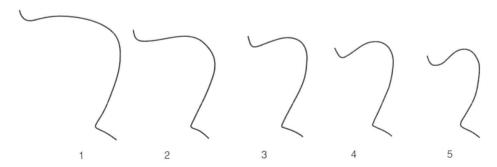

*Figure 8.2* Variation in the greater sciatic notch from (**1**) most feminine to (**5**) most masculine. Categories 3 and 4 are probably males with category 2 being indeterminate.

structure in females (arrow *1*); notice how this raised ridge of bone gently curves from the superiomedial corner of the anterior pubis, inferiorly and laterally to where it merges into the inferior part (called the ramus) of this bone. This gentle curve leaves the inferiomedial corner of the pubis untouched by the ventral arc (see arrow *2* in Figure 8.5a). In males, this structure is small or nonexistent (Figure 8.5a, *left*); when present, it follows the edge of the pubic bone so closely that it occupies the inferiomedial corner of the pubis.

The second structure observed by Phenice is the subpubic concavity of the ischiopubic ramus. This refers to the contour of the lower parts of the pubis and ischium, where it forms the subpubic angle, discussed earlier. Check this contour in the laboratory pelvis by turning the posterior side of the bone toward you. Is it concave (i.e., curves superiorly), or is it straight or slightly convex? See Figure 8.5b in the textbook for clarification. Lastly, view the medial edge of the pubic bone just below the pubic face. Is it relatively wide and dull (a male characteristic), or is it narrow and sharp (a female characteristic)? Use the bottom of Exercise Worksheet 8.1 to record your observations of the lab pelvis.

### Exercise 8.2: Attributing Sex Using Pelvic Metrics: Ischium–Pubic Index

In this exercise, you will learn how to take the ischium–pubic index. First, refer to Figure 8.3 in this manual to get an idea as to the measurements that need to be taken. The base point for both of these is inside the acetabulum (hip socket), where the ilium, ischium, and pubis fuse. Although difficult to see, this point is represented by a raised area, an irregularity, or a notch inside the acetabulum. A somewhat easier way of identifying this point is to view the scar where the pubis fused with the ilium and ischium, which is visible on the internal surface of the os coxa (see Figure 8.8 in the textbook). By placing your thumb on this area and pinching the bone with your index finger, the point inside the acetabulum can be obtained. Place one tip of a sliding caliper on that point in the hip socket, and swing the other to the end of the pubic bone and read the distance between the tips. Then, swing the tip on the pubic bone down to the bottom of the ischium and read the measurement. The index is obtained by dividing the pubic length by the ischium length, and multiplying the result by 100.

As described in the textbook, if the ancestral group is not known, index values below 84 are in the male range, while values above 94 are in the female range. The values between 84 and 94 can be used to attribute sex through a process that is too complex for a manual of this kind. If the ancestral group is known, different cutoff values are used. For Whites, index values under 91 are male, while any index over 94 is female; for Blacks, values under 84 are

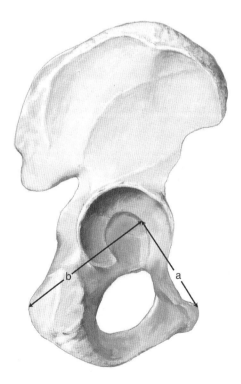

*Figure 8.3* Two measurements used for the ischiopubic index: (a) length of the pubis; (b) length of the ischium.

male, while indices over 91 are female. Again, values between these cutoff points can be used to attribute sex through a process too complex for this manual. Using this information, indicate the most likely sex of the individual in the space provided on Exercise Worksheet 8.2. Now, use all information gained from the lab pelvis (i.e., classic features, method of Phenice, and ischiopubic index value) to attribute sex. Enter your decision in the last space provided on Exercise Worksheet 8.2; and, in the comments area, enter your justification for making that determination. This is particularly important if the pelvis has characteristics that indicate both male and female or if there are oddities that make the attribution uncertain.

### Exercise 8.3: Attributing Sex Using Cranial Anthroposcopy

To determine the sex of a skull, review the information presented in the section Sexing the Skull as well as Table 8.3 and Figures 8.9 through 8.12 in the textbook. Also, study Figure 8.4 (in this manual) to better understand the variation in the skull characteristics used in sexing. Now, notice that the most basic differences between the skulls of males

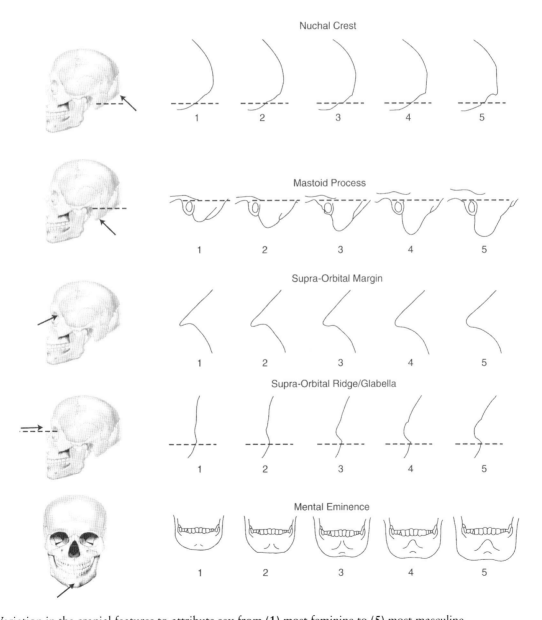

*Figure 8.4* Variation in the cranial features to attribute sex from (**1**) most feminine to (**5**) most masculine.

From Figure 4 of Buikstra JE and Ubelaker DH (1994) *Standards for Data Collection from Human Skeletal Remains*. Fayetteville, AR: Arkansas Archeological Survey Research Series #44. Reprinted with permission.

and females are size and rugosity; so, is the laboratory skull large and rugged, or small and smooth? Compare it to other skulls in the lab to help you make this basic distinction. Next, view the mastoid process; is it large and projecting (Figure 8.9a in the textbook and Figure 8.4 of this manual), or small and more of a bump than a process (Figure 8.9b)? Again, comparison with other lab skulls will help you make this distinction.

Next, observe the frontal (forehead) bone. Does it slope and have large browridges (Figure 8.10a in the textbook and Figure 8.4 in this manual), or is it more vertical with small or nonexistent browridges (Figure 8.10b in the textbook)? Turn the skull around and observe the backside, especially where the neck muscles attach. Is this nuchal area rugged with pronounced protuberances (Figure 8.11a in the textbook and Figure 8.4 in this manual), or smooth without projections (Figure 8.11b in the textbook)? Now, rub your thumb along the upper border of the eye, especially the superiolateral corner. Is the border sharp (a female characteristic), or blunt and rounded (a male characteristic)? Use Figure 8.4 in this manual to help make this determination. Finally, turn the mandible (lower jaw) over, and view the chin area from underneath. Is it broad and almost square as seen in Figure 8.12a of the textbook (male) or more pointed as in Figure 8.12b (female)? The drawings of the mental eminence in Figure 8.4 of this manual will help make this determination. Circle the appropriate expressions of your observations on the table in Exercise Worksheet 8.3, and enter your estimation of sex in the space provided.

As discussed in the textbook, the anthroposcopic traits of the skull can be used in logistic discriminant functions to assign sex. After completing the decision matrix on the top half of Exercise Worksheet 8.3, enter the numeric scores for the skull in the appropriate places on the bottom half of the worksheet and make the calculations. Ask the instructor the ancestral affiliation of the individual represented by the skull. Those values below zero (0) are male, while those above are female. Circle the indicated sex, and compare these results with the result entered on the top half of the worksheet. Discuss any discrepancies in the comments section of the worksheet.

## Exercise 8.4: Attributing Sex Using Cranial Metrics: Discriminant Functions

As with the pelvis, there are measurements of the skull that can help attribute sex. Table 8.1 in this manual presents descriptions of these measurements, and Figures 8.5, 8.6, and 8.7 present a graphical representation of these dimensions. Most of these measurements can be taken by holding the tips of sliding or spreading calipers to either end point and reading the measured distance. However, the length of the mastoid process is more problematic. Place a sliding caliper alongside of the skull with its jaws adjusted as in Figure 8.8 in this manual; be sure to hold the skull in the Frankfort plane (see Table 2.1 of the textbook for a definition) when taking this measurement.

Once taken, these dimensions can be entered on Exercise Worksheet 8.4 along with the coefficients of the appropriate discriminant functions presented in Tables 8.2, 8.3, and 8.4 of this manual for White, Black, and Asian skulls, respectively. Each measurement is multiplied by its coefficient, and all such calculations are summed to arrive at a function score. These scores are compared with the sectioning points in the tables to attribute sex. Function values below the sectioning point are female, while those above are male. Ask your instructor for the ancestral group of the laboratory skull before making any of the function calculations. Enter the sex in the space provided, and write the justification for your attribution in the comments area of the worksheet.

*Table 8.1* Definition of Measurements Used in Cranial Discriminant Functions

| Measurement | Definition |
| --- | --- |
| ML | Maximum length of the skull (Figure 8.5) |
| MB | Maximum breadth of the skull, above the supramastoid crest (Figure 8.6) |
| BaBr | Basion to Bregma (Figure 8.5) |
| BaNa | Basion to Nasion (Figure 8.5) |
| BB | Maximum width across the zygomatic arches (Figure 8.6) |
| BaPr | Basion to prosthion (Figure 8.7) |
| NaAl | Nasion to lowest point on the alveolar border between the central incisors (Figure 8.5) |
| PB | Maximum breadth of the palate (Figure 8.7) |
| LM | Length of the mastoid process while orienting the skull in the Frankfort plane; place the upper arm of the caliper in line with the upper border of the external auditory meatus while the lower arm is brought in line with the lowest point on the process while holding the caliper vertically (Figure 8.8) |

After Appendix to Giles (1970).

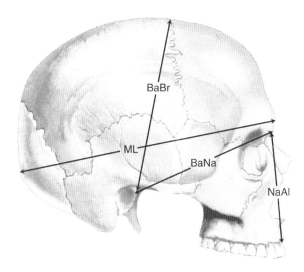

*Figure 8.5* Lateral view of the skull showing measurements used in discriminant functions.

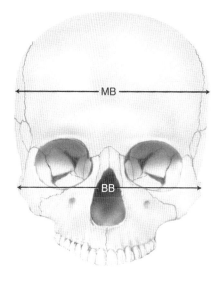

*Figure 8.6* Anterior view of the skull showing measurements used in discriminant functions.

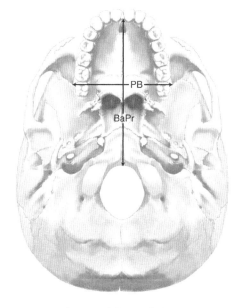

*Figure 8.7* Basal view of the skull showing measurements used in discriminant functions.

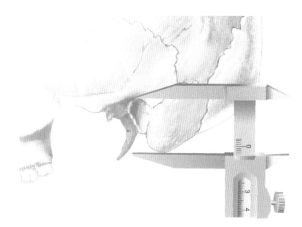

*Figure 8.8* Method for measuring the length of the mastoid process (LM).

From Figure 2, Sex determination by discriminant function analysis of crania, Giles E and Elliot O (1963) *American Journal of Physical Anthropology.* Reprinted by permission of Wiley-Liss, Inc., a subsidiary of John Wiley & Sons, Inc.

*Table 8.2* Discriminant Functions for Determining Sex of White Crania

| Measurement | Discriminant Function Number | | | | | |
| | 1 | 2 | 3 | 4 | 5 | 6 |
|---|---|---|---|---|---|---|
| ML | 3.107 | 3.400 | 1.800 | | 1.236 | 9.875 |
| MB | −4.643 | −3.833 | −1.783 | | −1.000 | |
| BaBr | 5.786 | 5.433 | 2.767 | | | |
| BaNa | | −0.167 | −0.100 | 10.714 | | 7.062 |
| BB | 14.821 | 12.200 | 6.300 | 16.381 | 3.291 | 19.062 |
| BaPr | 1.000 | −0.100 | | −1.000 | | −1.100 |
| NaAl | 2.714 | 2.200 | | 4.333 | | 4.375 |
| PB | −5.179 | | | −6.571 | | |
| LM | 6.071 | 5.367 | 2.833 | 14.810 | 1.528 | |
| **Section point** | 2672.39 | 2592.32 | 1296.20 | 3348.27 | 536.93 | 5066.69 |
| **Percentage correct** | 86.6 | 86.4 | 86.4 | 84.5 | 85.5 | 84.9 |

From Table LI in Giles (1970).

*Table 8.3* Discriminant Functions for Determining Sex of Black Crania

| Measurement | Discriminant Function Number | | | | | |
| | 7 | 8 | 9 | 10 | 11 | 12 |
| --- | --- | --- | --- | --- | --- | --- |
| ML | 9.222 | 3.895 | 3.533 | | 2.111 | 2.867 |
| MB | 7.000 | 3.632 | 1.667 | | 1.000 | |
| BaBr | 1.000 | 1.000 | 0.867 | | | |
| BaNa | | −2.053 | 0.100 | 1.000 | | −0.100 |
| BB | 31.111 | 12.947 | 8.700 | 19.389 | 4.936 | 12.367 |
| BaPr | 5.889 | 1.368 | | 2.778 | | −0.233 |
| NaAl | 20.222 | 8.158 | | 11.778 | | 6.900 |
| PB | −30.556 | | | −14.333 | | |
| LM | 47.111 | 19.947 | 4.367 | 23.667 | 8.037 | |
| Section point | 8171.53 | 4079.12 | 2515.91 | 3461.46 | 1387.72 | 2568.97 |
| Percentage correct | 87.6 | 86.6 | 86.5 | 87.5 | 85.3 | 85.0 |

From Table LI in Giles (1970).

*Table 8.4* Discriminant Functions for Determining Sex of Asian Crania

| Measurement | 13 | 14 |
| --- | --- | --- |
| ML | 1.000 | 1.000 |
| MB | −0.062 | 0.221 |
| BaBr | 1.865 | |
| BB | 1.257 | 1.095 |
| NaAl | | 0.504 |
| Section point | 579.96 | 380.84 |
| Percentage correct | 86.4 | 83.1 |

Taken from Table LI of Giles (1970) for Japanese.

## Exercise 8.5: Attributing Sex Using Postcranial Metrics

The measurements of some postcranial bones can be used to a limited extent to attribute sex. Take the maximum length of the scapula by measuring the straight distance between the superior and inferior borders (see Figure 8.9a of this manual); values of less than 14 centimeters indicate female, while values of 17 centimeters and over indicate males. Next, measure the height of the glenoid cavity (see Figure 8.9b); measurements above 36 millimeters generally are male (due

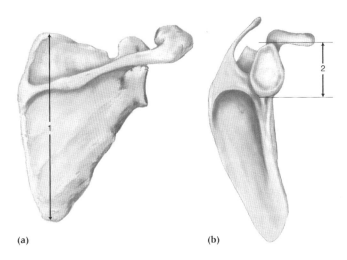

(a)                    (b)

*Figure 8.9* Measurements of the scapula used to estimate sex: (**a**) height of the scapula (*line 1*); (**b**) height of the glenoid cavity (*line 2*).

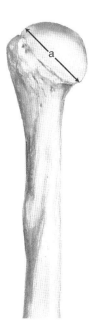

*Figure 8.10* Vertical head diameter measurement of the humerus (*line a*).

*Figure 8.11* Measurement of the radial head. The maximum diameter is the greatest value of distance (*line a*) when rotating the radius 360°. The minimum diameter is the least value when the bone is rotated.

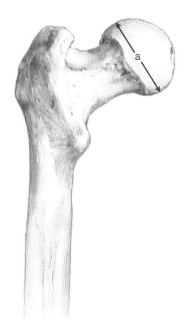

*Figure 8.12* Head diameter of the femur (*line a*).

*Table 8.5* Sexing From the Femoral Head Diameter

| Ancestral Group | Female | Probable Female | Indeterminate Sex | Probable Male | Male |
|---|---|---|---|---|---|
| White[1] | Under 42.5 | 42.5–43.5 | 43.5–46.5 | 46.5–47.5 | Over 47.5 |
| Black[2] | Under 40 | 40–43 | 43–44 | 44–47 | Over 47 |

1   From data presented by Stewart (1979).
2   From data presented by Bass (1995).

to the larger size of the humeral head), while those below are female. Also, measure the vertical diameter of the head of the humerus (see Figure 8.10 of this manual), the radius (see Figure 8.11 of this manual), and of the femur (see Figure 8.12 of this manual). Humeral values below 43 millimeters almost certainly represent a female. Measurements from 43 to 44 are probably female, while values 46 to 47 are probably male. Measurements over 47 millimeters are almost certainly male. Maximum radial head values of 21 millimeters or less are likely female, while values of 24 millimeters or more are likely male. The values for minimum radial head diameter are 20 and 23 millimeters, respectively. For femoral values, consult Table 8.5 in this manual; notice that the ancestry of the skeleton must be known to use this measurement. Place an *X* in the appropriate column of Exercise Worksheet 8.5 for male or female using the sectioning points for these measurements. If the values indicate probable male or probable female, use the male or female column as appropriate.

Now add the number of *X*'s in each column of Exercise Worksheet 8.5, and place the total on the bottom line. The column with the most *X*'s represents the most probable sex of the lab skeleton. (These last measurements are not considered as accurate as the index and discriminant functions in Exercise Worksheets 8.2 and 8.4; thus, disagreements between these two methods should favor the functions.) Again, write the justification of your attribution in the comments area of the worksheet.

## NOTE TO INSTRUCTORS

It would be difficult to offer this lab without pelvises and skulls of both sexes. Fortunately, inexpensive casts can be obtained from the sources described in the Sources of Materials section of this manual. As stated, I can personally vouch for the budget male and female pelvises of Carolina Biological Supply, which show both the classic features of each of the sexes as well as the characteristics of Phenice. In addition, judging from the picture on its website, the female skull appears to illustrate the characteristics of that sex.

## Exercise Worksheet 8.1: Attributing Sex Using Pelvic Anthroposcopy

Name: _____    Date: _____

Case/Accession number: _____

### General Sex Characteristics

| Trait | Males | Females |
|---|---|---|
| Size | Large and rugged | Small and gracile |
| Ilium | High and vertical | Low and flat |
| Pelvic inlet | Heart-shaped | Circular or elliptical |
| Pubic shape | Narrow, rectangular | Broad, square |
| Subpubic angle | V-shaped | U-shaped |
| Obturator foramen | Large, ovoid | Small, triangular |
| Greater sciatic notch | Narrow | Wide |
| Preauricular sulcus | Small or absent | Well-developed |
| Shape of sacrum | Long and narrow | Short and broad |
| Total | _____ | _____ |

After Table 37 of Krogman (1962).

Sex: _____

### Characteristics of Phenice

| Trait | Males | Females |
|---|---|---|
| Ventral arc | Absent/Small | Present/Large |
| Subpubic concavity | Absent | Present |
| Medial aspect of ischiopubic ramus | Wide/Dull | Narrow/Sharp |
| Total | _____ | _____ |

After Phenice (1969).

Sex: _____

**Exercise Worksheet 8.2: Attributing Sex Using Pelvic Metrics: Ischium–Pubic Index**

Name: _____ Date: _____

Case/Accession number: _____

_____ ÷ _____ × 100 = _____
(Pubic length)    (Ischium length)

Sex:_____

Sex (from all sources):_____

Comments: _____

_____

_____

## Exercise Worksheet 8.3: Attributing Sex Using Cranial Anthroposcopy

Name: _____   Date: _____

Case/Accession number: _____

### Characteristics of Male and Female Skulls

| Traits | Males | Females |
|---|---|---|
| Size | Large and rugged | Small and smooth |
| Mastoid | Large, projecting | Small, nonprojecting |
| Browridges | Large | Small, none |
| Frontal | Slanted | High, rounded |
| Nuchal area | Rugged with hook | Smooth, hook uncommon |
| Supraorbital margin | Rounded | Sharp |
| Chin | Broad | Pointed |
| **Total Count** | _____ | _____ |

Summarized from France (1998) and Krogman (1962).

Sex: _____

## Modern Populations*

9.128 – 1.375 (_____) – 1.185 (_____) – 1.151 (_____) = _____      Male      Female
$\qquad$ Glabella $\qquad$ Mastoid $\qquad$ Mental

7.434 – 1.568 (_____) – 1.459 (_____) = _____      Male      Female
$\qquad$ Glabella $\qquad$ Mastoid

7.372 – 1.525 (_____) – 1.485 (_____) = _____      Male      Female
$\qquad$ Glabella $\qquad$ Mental

7.382 – 1.629 (_____) – 1.415 (_____) = _____      Male      Female
$\qquad$ Mental $\qquad$ Mastoid

6.018 – 1.007 (_____) – 1.850 (_____) = _____      Male      Female
$\qquad$ Orbital margin $\qquad$ Mental

5.329 – 0.7 (_____) – 1.559 (_____) = _____      Male      Female
$\qquad$ Nuchal $\qquad$ Mastoid

**Native Americans\***

3.414 − 0.499 (_____) − 0.606 (_____) = _____     Male     Female
$\phantom{3.414 - 0.499 (}$ Orbital margin $\phantom{) - 0.606 (}$ Mental

4.765 − 0.576 (_____) − 1.136 (_____) = _____     Male     Female
$\phantom{4.765 - 0.576 (}$ Mental $\phantom{) - 1.136 (}$ Mastoid

5.025 − 0.797 (_____) − 1.085 (_____) = _____     Male     Female
$\phantom{5.025 - 0.797 (}$ Glabella $\phantom{) - 1.085 (}$ Mastoid

*Coefficients from Walker (2008).

**Comments:** _____

_____

_____

_____

**Exercise Worksheet 8.4: Attributing Sex Using Cranial Metrics: Discriminant Functions**

Name: _____  Date: _____

Case/Accession number: _____

Max length (ML)          _____  ×  _____  =  _____
                                            (coefficient)

Max breadth (MB)         _____  ×  _____  =  _____
                                            (coefficient)

Basion–bregma (BaBr)     _____  ×  _____  =  _____
                                            (coefficient)

Basion–nasion (BaNa)     _____  ×  _____  =  _____
                                            (coefficient)

Bizygomatic breadth (BB) _____  ×  _____  =  _____
                                            (coefficient)

Basion–prosthion (BaPr)  _____  ×  _____  =  _____
                                            (coefficient)

Nasion–alveolare (NaAl)  _____  ×  _____  =  _____
                                            (coefficient)

Palatal breadth (PB)     _____  ×  _____  =  _____
                                            (coefficient)

Mastoid length (LM)      _____  ×  _____  =  _____
                                            (coefficient)

Sum: _____

Sectioning point: _____

Sex: _____

Comments: _____
_____
_____

**Exercise Worksheet 8.5: Attributing Sex Using Postcranial Metrics**

Name: _____   Date: _____

Case/Accession number: _____

| Bone | Measurement | Sex | | |
| --- | --- | --- | --- | --- |
| | | *Male* | *Unknown* | *Female* |
| Scapula | | | | |
|   Body | _____ | _____ | _____ | _____ |
|   Glenoid fossa | _____ | _____ | _____ | _____ |
| Head of humerus | _____ | _____ | _____ | _____ |
| Head of radius | _____ | _____ | _____ | _____ |
| Head of femur | _____ | _____ | _____ | _____ |
| **Total count** | | _____ | _____ | _____ |

Sex: _____

Sex (from all sources): _____

Comments: _____

_____

_____

# 9   Estimation of Age at Death

The estimation of age at death is the third demographic characteristic that can be discerned from skeletal remains. In subadults, methods for approximating this parameter are based on the growing skeleton and dentition, while the age of adult skeletons can be ascertained from traits of the deteriorating skeleton. The first part of this lab deals with assigning age to the skeletons of persons approximately 18 years old or younger using long limb bone lengths, tooth eruption, and epiphyseal union. The second part deals with methods for estimating the age of adults from changes in the pubic faces, auricular surface of the os coxa, sternal rib ends, and cranial suture closure.

## Learning Objectives

During this lab session, you will learn how to estimate the age at death of persons from their skeletal remains. If your lab has examples, you will learn this on both subadult and adult skeletons.

## Expected Outcomes

By the end of this lab session, you will be able to:

- Estimate age at death of subadults from long limb bone measurements.
- Estimate age at death of subadults from observations of dental eruption.
- Estimate age at death of subadults from epiphyseal union and centers of ossification.
- Estimate age at death of adults from changes in the pubic faces.
- Estimate age at death of adults from changes in the auricular surface of the os coxa.
- Estimate age at death of adults from the configuration of sternal rib ends.
- Estimate age at death of adults from cranial and palatal suture closure.

## Minimum Materials

Os coxa from an adult human

## Optional Materials

Skull from an adult
Subadult skeleton, including long limb bone(s), jaws, and teeth

## SUBADULTS

As in the textbook, this section is divided into four categories, one for each of the ways that the age at death of subadults can be estimated. Depending on the material available in your lab, some of these may have to be omitted.

### Exercise 9.1: Estimating Age at Death Using Long Limb Bone Measurements

Before commencing this analysis, familiarize yourself with the information concerning age at death and long limb bone measurements as described in the section Long Bone Lengths in the textbook. If you have access to the skeleton of a child who was under the age of 13 at death, measure the lengths (without the epiphyseal ends) of all of the long bones

*Table 9.1* Determining Length of Femur From Other Long Bones

| Bone | Multiplier |
| --- | --- |
| Tibia | 1.11 |
| Fibula | 1.18 |
| Humerus | 1.13 |
| Ulna | 1.18 |
| Radius | 1.36 |

Based on data calculated from Figures 29 and 30 of Stewart (1979).

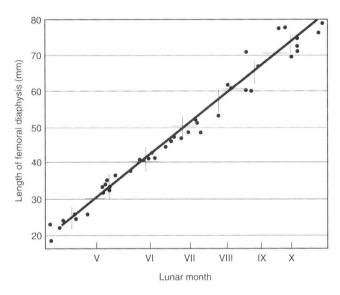

*Figure 9.1* Relationship between femoral shaft length and fetal age.
Modified from Figure 36, Stewart (1979, p. 129).

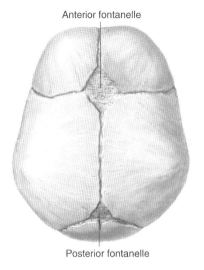

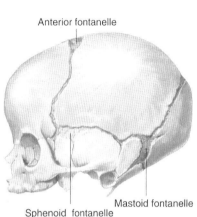

*Figure 9.2* Placement of fontanelles in the infant skull.

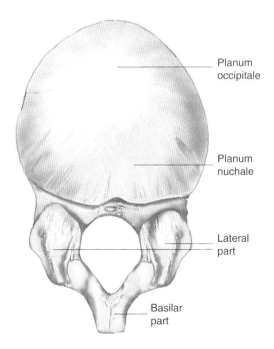

*Figure 9.3* Primary centers of ossification seen in the occipital.

that are present using a sliding caliper or bone board. Now, use Figures 9.1 through 9.7 in the textbook to estimate age at death by finding the bone length on the vertical axis of the figures and determining the concomitant age from the horizontal axis. If you have multiple bones, complete a range chart (see Chapter 1 in the textbook for a description) on Exercise Worksheet 9.1, and determine the best estimate of age from the area of greatest overlap between the different bones. (This chart is arranged horizontally on the worksheet instead of vertically as in the textbook.)

If any of the lengths of these bones is less than the minimum values found on the figures and the femur is not present, use the information in Table 9.1 of this manual to determine the length of the femur that would be associated with these bones. Then, use Figure 9.1 of this manual to estimate age at death. For example, if a radius is 42 millimeters long, multiply that value by 1.36 to arrive at an estimate of femoral length (in this case, 42 × 1.36 = 57 millimeters). Then compare the result with Figure 9.1 of this manual to arrive at an estimate of age (in this case, approximately the eighth month in utero).

*Table 9.2* Fusion of Primary Centers of Ossification

| Site | Time of Closure |
|---|---|
| *Fontanelles* | |
| Spheonoid and mastoid | Soon after birth |
| Posterior | During first year |
| Anterior | During second year |
| *Mandible* | |
| Right and left halves | Completed by second year |
| *Frontal* | |
| Right and left halves | In second year (remains open in as many as 10% of people) |
| *Atlas* | |
| Union of posterior halves | In third year |
| Union of anterior halves | In sixth year |
| *Axis* | |
| Dens, body, and both arches | In third and fourth years |
| *Occipital* | |
| Squamous with lateral parts | In fifth year |
| Lateral and basilar parts | In sixth year |

Taken from data in Stewart (1979).

## Exercise 9.2: Estimating Age at Death Using Union of Primary Ossification Centers

Before commencing this analysis, familiarize yourself with the information concerning age at death and ossification centers as described in the section Union of Primary Ossification Centers in the textbook. If you have access to the skeleton of a child who died before reaching the age of 7, use the information in Figures 9.2 and 9.3 and Table 9.2 in this manual to estimate age at death. First, identify the bones of the skull as well as the ossification centers of the occipital. Now, determine the states of union seen in these bones, and note them on Exercise Worksheet 9.2 by circling all states that are applicable to each bone fusion. Using this as a decision matrix, make the best estimate of age at death of the lab skeleton.

## Exercise 9.3: Estimating Age at Death Using Tooth Formation and Eruption

Before commencing this analysis, familiarize yourself with the information in the Tooth Formation and Tooth Eruption sections in the textbook. To estimate age using degree of tooth formation, radiographs of dentition are needed. If you have access to such information, compare each tooth with the developmental stages given in Figure 9.4 of this manual and their coding in Table 9.3. Be sure to distinguish between single-rooted teeth (i.e., incisors, canine, and many premolars) and multiple-rooted teeth (i.e., some premolars and all molars). Also, the $C_i$ stage (initial cusp formation) is not used when viewing deciduous teeth; and, similarly, the $Cl_i$ stage (initial cleft formation) is not applicable to single-rooted teeth. In addition, schedules of tooth formation for deciduous teeth are available only for the mandibular canines and molars.

Ask the lab instructor the sex and ancestry of the skeleton you are studying, and match up the stage of development in each tooth with information presented in Figures 9.11 and 9.12 as well as Tables 9.3 and 9.4 in the textbook, whichever is applicable. If sex and ancestry are not known (a very likely situation in a forensic case), use the data on both sexes and ancestral groups for this analysis. Now, on Exercise Worksheet 9.3, create a range chart showing the limits of 95% of the values for each age as well as the means (also called averages) of all of the teeth for which you have information. These statistics are already given for the three deciduous teeth in Figures 9.11 and 9.12 in the textbook. For permanent teeth, create these limits by multiplying the standard deviations (SD) given in the textbook's Tables 9.3 and 9.4 by 2. If sex and ancestry are not known, add this value to the highest mean for the stage of development, and subtract it from the lowest mean for that stage of development. This will give you a conservative age range estimate. For example, if the permanent maxillary central incisor of a lab jaw is in stage 9 ($R_{1/4}$), then two times the SD (Tables 9.3 and 9.4 in the textbook) is $0.82 \times 2 = 1.64$ years. To calculate where 95% of children with this stage of

(a) Single-rooted teeth

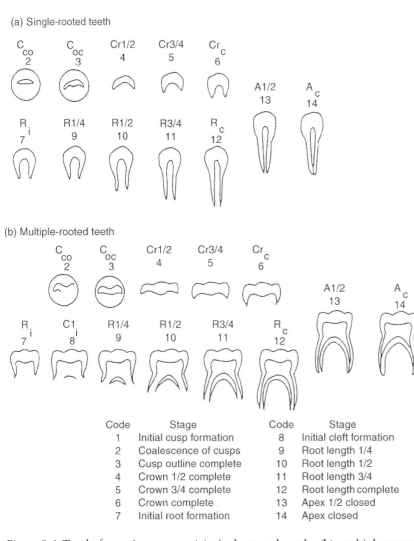

(b) Multiple-rooted teeth

| Code | Stage | Code | Stage |
|------|-------|------|-------|
| 1 | Initial cusp formation | 8 | Initial cleft formation |
| 2 | Coalescence of cusps | 9 | Root length 1/4 |
| 3 | Cusp outline complete | 10 | Root length 1/2 |
| 4 | Crown 1/2 complete | 11 | Root length 3/4 |
| 5 | Crown 3/4 complete | 12 | Root length complete |
| 6 | Crown complete | 13 | Apex 1/2 closed |
| 7 | Initial root formation | 14 | Apex closed |

*Table 9.3* Coding of Stages of Tooth Development in Single- and Multiple-Rooted Teeth

| | Numeric Codes | |
|---|---|---|
| *Stage* | *Single-Rooted* | *Multiple-Rooted* |
| $C_1$ | 1 | 1 |
| $C_{CO}$ | 2 | 2 |
| $C_{OC}$ | 3 | 3 |
| $Cr_{1/2}$ | 4 | 4 |
| $Cr_{3/4}$ | 5 | 5 |
| $Cr_C$ | 6 | 6 |
| $R_1$ | 7 | 7 |
| $Cl_1$ | N/A | 8 |
| $R_{1/4}$ | 9 | 9 |
| $R_{1/2}$ | 10 | 10 |
| $R_{3/4}$ | 11 | 11 |
| $R_C$ | 12 | 12 |
| $A_{1/2}$ | 13 | 13 |
| $A_C$ | 14 | 14 |

*Figure 9.4* Tooth formation stages: (**a**) single-rooted teeth; (**b**) multiple-rooted teeth.

Reprinted from Moorrees et al. (1963) Age variation of formation stages for ten permanent teeth, *American Journal of Physical Anthropology.* Copyright © 1963, John Wiley & Sons. Reprinted with permission of Wiley-Liss, Inc. a subsidiary of John Wiley & Sons, Inc.

development fall, add this value to the highest mean (i.e., since White males have the highest mean, add 1.64 to 7.5 getting 9.14 years) to find the high end of the age range. Subtract the 2 × SD value from the lowest mean (i.e., since Black females have the lowest mean, the calculation is 6.4 – 1.64 = 4.76 years) to find the low end of the age range. To estimate the average, add the four means (White male, Black male, White female, Black female) and divide by 4 (i.e., [7.5 + 7.2 + 6.9 + 6.4] ÷ 4 = 7). These would be sketched on the chart as:

Do this for all teeth seen in the radiograph. When you have completed this chart, the best age-at-death estimate is the area of greatest overlap between the oldest limits drawn on the chart (i.e., if both deciduous and permanent teeth are present, use only the permanent teeth limits). Once this is determined, enter that estimate in the space provided.

To estimate the age at death from tooth eruption, simply compare the dentition of the lab skull with Figures 9.5 and 9.6 of this manual. If the ancestry is not known or is known to be Black, combine the two estimates in the same manner as discussed earlier for tooth formation. Pay careful attention to the deciduous versus permanent teeth. Note the age so determined, and include the appropriate plus/minus figure to indicate the 95% certainty range, on the worksheet.

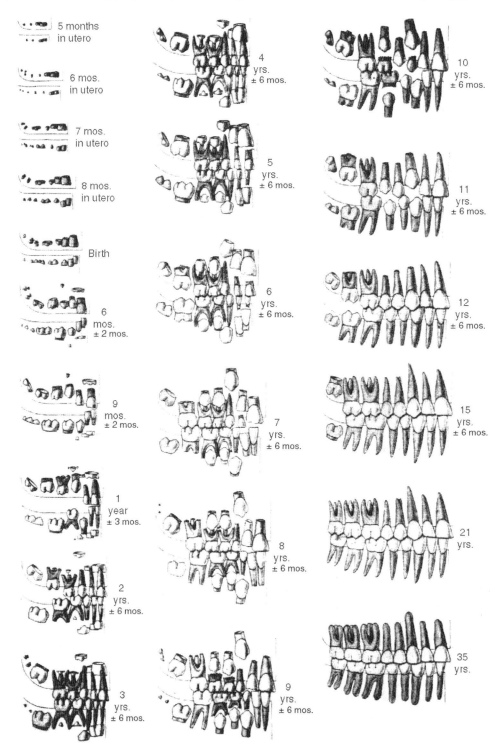

*Figure 9.5* Chart of tooth formation and emergence for White children.

Adapted from Schour I and Massler M, The development of human dentition, *JADA* 1941; 28: 1153. Copyright © 1941 American Dental Association. Reprinted by permission of ADA Publishing, a division of ADA Business Enterprises, Inc.

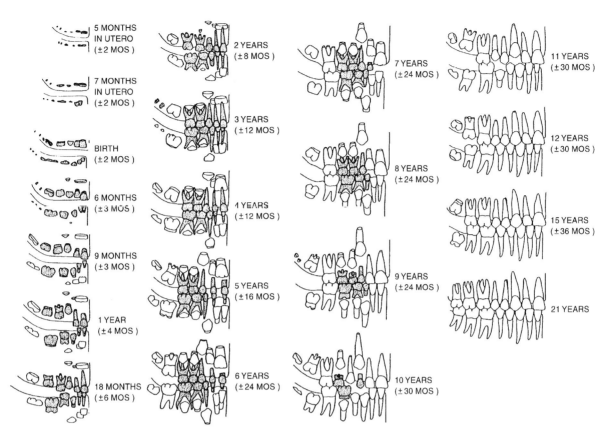

*Figure 9.6* Chart of tooth formation and emergence for Native American children.

Reprinted from Figure 71, Ubelaker (1999); courtesy of Taraxacum Press.

## Exercise 9.4: Estimating Age at Death Using Epiphyseal Union

Before attempting to estimate age by epiphyseal union, familiarize yourself with this concept by studying Figure 9.7 of this manual and reading the section Epiphyseal Union in Chapter 9 of the textbook. Now, starting at the superior end of the vertebral column, look at each vertebra and determine if the two halves of the neural arch are fused and if the arch is fused to the centrum (body). Next, observe the humeri; are the various epiphyses fused, and if so, are the lines still visible? Continue this process through all of the limb bones as well as the scapula and pelvis. Finally, view the sacrum and spheno-occipital synchondrosis (the area of attachment between the two sections of the basilar part of the occipital bone).

As with earlier exercises, develop a range chart on Exercise Worksheet 9.4 from limits given in Figure 9.16 of the textbook, and use the area of greatest overlap to determine the best age estimate. As an example, suppose a male humerus and femur are found with varying amounts of epiphyseal union. The distal epiphysis and medial epicondyle of the humerus are fully fused, but the head is only partially fused. Using an abbreviated chart from Worksheet 9.4 (see below), there would be a line extending from around 17 years of age for each of the first two structures (indicating the minimum age of the person based on the humerus), and a bar extending from around 14 to 24 years of age for the head. The right end of this line sets the upper limit (ca. 24 years) for the age of this individual. Viewing the femur, the greater trochanter is fully fused (line extending from 19 years), as are the head and lesser trochanter (another line extending from 19 years on); both of these set the lower limit of this person's age at around 19 years. Finally, the distal epiphysis is still fusing (line from 14 to 21), indicating an age no greater than 21 years. From this information, the area of greatest overlap is 19 to 21 years of age for all six epiphyses. (When reporting this figure to law enforcement, it is advisable that an age of late teens to early 20s be cited because 19 to 21 is more precise than is warranted considering variations, not pictured in Figure 9.16 of the textbook, in the timing of epiphyseal union.)

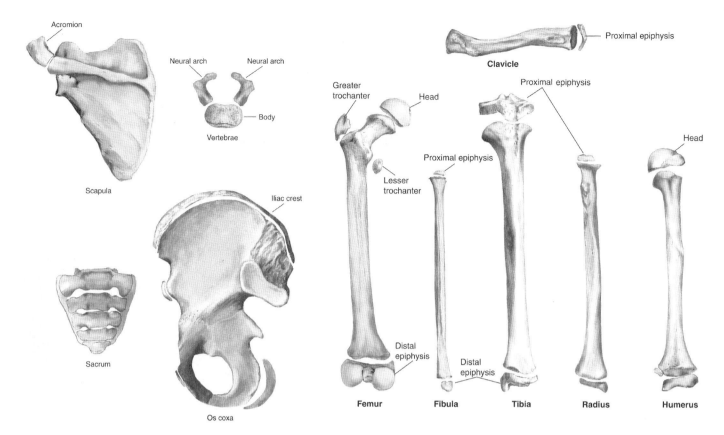

*Figure 9.7* Epiphyseal union of various bones.

Humerus (head)

Humerus (medial epicondyle)

Humerus (distal epiphysis)

Femur (greater trochanter)

Femur (head, lesser trochanter)

Femur (distal epiphysis)

## ADULTS

As in the textbook, this part of the lab is divided into four categories, one for each of the anthroposcopic ways in which the age at death can be estimated in adults. Again, not all of these may be possible with the materials available in your lab.

### Exercise 9.5: Estimating Age at Death Using Symphyseal Surface

To estimate age from changes in the symphyseal surface, first acquaint yourself with the features used for this purpose: the pubic face, the ventral and dorsal margins, and the upper and lower extremities (Figure 9.8 of this manual). Also, read the section Symphyseal Surface in the textbook. Now, check the pubic face of the lab pelvis. Are there ridges separated by furrows running transversely across the surface (see Figure 9.17a in the textbook)? If the ridges exist, are their tops sharp and the furrows V-shaped, or are both of these features more rounded (see Figure 9.17b in the textbook)? If there are few or no ridges and furrows, is the face flat with a fine-grained look to the bone, as in Figure 9.17c, or is it more granular as in Figure 9.17d, or is it pitted and eroded as in Figure 9.17e?

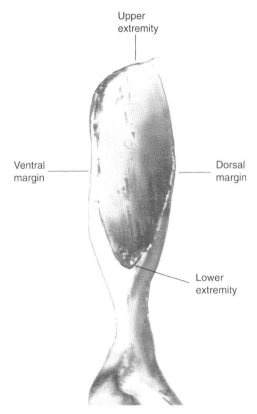

*Figure 9.8* Major components of the symphyseal surface used to estimate age at death.

Next, look at the ventral (anterior) margin of the pubic face. Does it form a right angle with the pubic face (see Figure 9.18a of the textbook), or is there more of a bevel between the face and the anterior surface of the pubis (see Figure 9.18b)? If the ventral margin is more rounded, is this caused by a bevel or a deposit of new bone (called the rampart; see Figures 9.18c and 9.18d in the textbook)? Now, look at the dorsal margin. Does the pubic surface curve toward it as in *1* of Figure 9.19a, or is the margin built up, causing the surface to extend backward into a plateau (see *2* of Figure 9.19a in the textbook)?

Now, view the upper and lower margins (extremities) of the pubic face. Are their edges easily distinguishable, or does the bone of the pubic face blend with both the inferior and superior surfaces of the pubis (see *1, 2,* and *3* of Figure 9.19b in the textbook)? Finally, look for the last three features of this bone. First, are there "blobs" of bone (called ossific nodules) on the pubic surface (see Figure 9.20a in the textbook)? Second, is there a rim encircling the pubic face as in Figure 9.20b? Last, is there lipping of the ventral and dorsal margins?

Assess each feature of the pubic face of the lab pelvis and, on the table in Exercise Worksheet 9.5, circle the appropriate stage of modification for each (some stages span several phases). Now determine the sex of the pelvis using the traits learned in Chapter 8 of the textbook and this lab manual (or obtain the sex from the lab instructor). When finished, establish the most likely age of the lab individual by determining the row with the most circles, and comparing the phase of that row with the age ranges in Table 9.6 in the textbook. If two rows have equal numbers, the most likely age is the average of the two means. For example, if there are equal numbers of circles in Phase IV and Phase V, the most likely age is in the low 40s, if the pelvis is female, and around 40 years of age if male.

## Exercise 9.6: Estimating Age at Death Using Auricular Surface of the Os Coxae

Before commencing this analysis, familiarize yourself with the information concerning age at death and auricular surface changes as described in the section Auricular Surface of the Os Coxae in the textbook. To estimate age from changes to this structure, first acquaint yourself with the areas of the ilium used for this purpose: the auricular surface, its apex, and the retroauricular area (see Figure 9.9 of this manual). Now, look at the five features of these areas that change with age. View the bone of the auricular surface. Is it formed into billows (see *1* of Figure 9.22a in the textbook), or is the surface covered with striae (see *2* of Figure 9.22a), or are there no lines traversing the surface (see *3* of Figure 9.22a)?

Next, view the texture of the bone on the auricular surface. Is this bone granular (see *2* of Figure 9.22b in the textbook), coarse (see *1* of Figure 9.22b), or dense, or has it begun to degenerate? Then, look at the porosity of the auricular surface bone. If porosity is present, is it composed of small perforations (microporosity; see *1* of Figure 9.23a), or is it large (macroporosity; see *2* of Figure 9.23a)?

Now, view the retroauricular area. Is the bone of this region smooth and youthful looking (see *1* of Figure 9.23b) or more coarse (see *2* of Figure 9.23b), or does it exhibit osteophytes and other outgrowths (see *3* of Figure 9.23b)? Finally, view the apex; does it have a thin crescent border (Figure 9.24a), or is it thick (Figure 9.24b)?

Use the table in Exercise Worksheet 9.6 to assess each of the features described here. Circle the appropriate expression on the table and determine the row with the most circles. Again, the best estimate of age is derived from the row with the most number of circles.

*Figure 9.9* Major components of the posterior ilium used in determining age.

## Exercise 9.7: Estimating Age at Death Using Sternal Rib Ends

Before commencing this analysis, familiarize yourself with the information concerning age at death and sternal rib end changes as described in the section Sternal Rib Ends in the textbook. To estimate age from changes in these bones, first acquaint yourself with the features of the rib ends used for this purpose: surface bone, surface contour, rim edge, and rim contour. Now, view each of these on the lab's rib ends. Is the surface bone smooth as in *1* of Figure 9.25a in the textbook, granular as in *2* of Figure 9.25a, or porous as in *3* of Figure 9.25a? Now, view the contour of the bone on the rib's end. Is this surface billowy (see *1* of Figure 9.25b in the textbook), flat (see *2* of Figure 9.25b), indented with a V-shape (see *3* of Figure 9.25b), or indented with a U-shape (see *4* of Figure 9.25b)?

Next, view the rim around the sternal end. Is the edge of the rim rounded (see *1* of Figure 9.25c in the textbook), or thin with a jagged edge (see *2* of Figure 9.25c)? Finally, look at the contour of the rim viewed from the side. Is the rim fairly straight, with contour only supplied by the coarseness of the bone (see *1* of Figure 9.25d in the textbook) or wavy (see *2* of Figure 9.25d), or are there fingers of bone extending out from the rim (see *3* of Figure 9.25d)? (In some cases, the end of the bone will flare outward, making the end of the rib wider than the body.)

Use the table in Exercise Worksheet 9.7 to assess each of the features described here for the rib ends. Circle the appropriate expressions in the table and count the circles in each row. Again, the best estimate of age is derived from the row with the highest number of circles.

## Exercise 9.8: Estimating Age at Death Using Cranial Suture Closure

Before attempting to estimate age from suture closure, read the section Cranial Suture Closure in the textbook, and review Figure 9.26 to familiarize yourself with the four stages of closure: open, partial, significant, and obliterated. Now, view Figure 9.10 and Table 9.4 of this manual for the 10 locations on the cranial vault that are particularly useful for determining age. Score each of these sites for the degree of closure by observing a 1-centimeter area around each point. Use a 0 for no closure, 1 for partial, 2 for significant, and 3 for obliterated. Enter these figures on Exercise Worksheet 9.8, and then add them together to obtain a total score. Now, using Table 9.5 of this manual, determine the appropriate stage (S1 to S6) and compare that stage with Figure 9.11 of this manual to get the most likely age. Enter that age, and its concomitant range, on the worksheet.

Now, view the sutures of the endocranial area (Figure 9.12 of this manual) for the amount of closure. Observe these either through the foramen magnum using a pen light for illumination, or directly on the top of the skull that was removed during autopsy. If there is minimal (or less) closure at the three sites, the age is between 20 and 34 years. If there is significant closure at the sites, then an age of 35 to 49 is indicated. Lastly, if the sutures are obliterated, an age of 50 years and over is most likely.

Finally, if the palate is present on the lab skull, view its sutures for degree of closure. Using Figure 9.13 of this manual, review the section Palatal Sutures in the textbook to help you identify the three sutures in the palatal area

*Table 9.4* Sites on the Ectocranium Used for Age Determination

| Site | Definition |
| --- | --- |
| Midlambdoid | Midpoint on lambdoid suture (usually observed on left side) |
| Lambda | Area around lambda |
| Obelion | Area between the parietal foramen |
| Anterior-sagittal | Area at vertex of skull when held in Frankfort horizon; usually 1/3 distance from bregma to lambda |
| Bregma | Area around bregma |
| Midcoronal | Area approximately 2/3 of the distance from bregma to pterion |
| Pterion | Meeting of the sphenoid with the frontal and parietal |
| Sphenofrontal | Area between greater wing of the sphenoid and frontal |
| Inferior sphenotemporal | Area opposite the glenoid fossa on the sphenotemporal suture |
| Superior sphenotemporal | Area on the sphenotemporal suture superior to the zygomatic arch |

Summarized from Table 1 of Meindl and Lovejoy (1985).

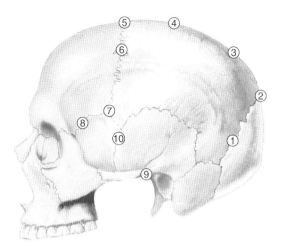

*Figure 9.10* Vault sites used in estimating age from ectocranial suture closure.

*Table 9.5* Composite Scores of Vault and Lateral–Anterior Sutures

| Composite Score | Stage | Composite Score | Stage |
|---|---|---|---|
| 1–2 | S1 | 1 | S1 |
| 3–6 | S2 | 2 | S2 |
| 7–11 | S3 | 3–5 | S3 |
| 12–15 | S4 | 6 | S4 |
| 16–18 | S5 | 7–8 | S5 |
| 19–20 | S6 | 9–10 | S6 |
| | | 11–14 | S7 |

From Buikstra JE and Ubelaker DH (1994) *Standards for Data Collection from Human Skeletal Remains.* Fayetteville AR: Arkansas Archaeological Survey Research Series #44. Reprinted by permission.

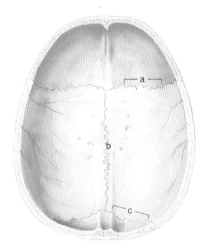

*Figure 9.12* Endocranial suture locations: (**a**) area between bregma and pterion; (**b**) sagittal suture; (**c**) segment from lambda to asterion on the lambdoid suture.

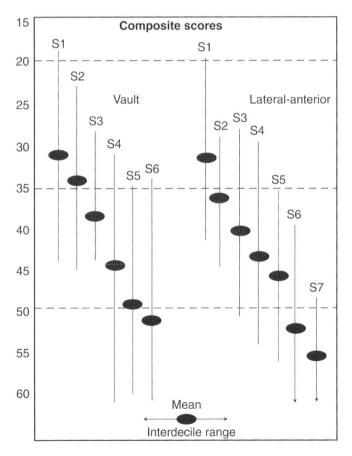

*Figure 9.11* Chart showing relationship between closure scores and age.

From Buikstra JE and Ubelaker DH (1994) *Standards for Data Collection from Human Skeletal Remains.* Fayetteville AR: Arkansas Archaeological Survey Research Series #44. Reprinted by Permission.

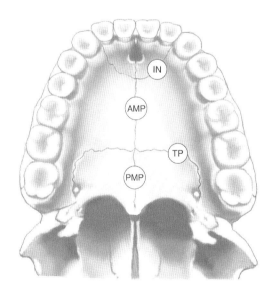

*Figure 9.13* Sutures and sites of the palate used for determining age: incisive suture (**IN**), median palatine (**AMP**, **PMP**), transverse palatine (**TP**).

used in this method: incisive, median palatine, and transverse palatine. If there is complete closure of the incisive suture (IN) as well as partial closure of the Posterior Median Palatine (PMP) and Transverse Palatine (TP) areas, then an age of 20 to 32 years is indicated. If there is complete closure at these same three areas and the anterior part of the Anterior Median Palatine (AMP) is partially open, then an age of 33 to 50 is indicated. Finally, complete obliteration of all sutures is indicative of over 50 years of age.

## NOTE TO INSTRUCTORS

Offering this lab session can be challenging because skeletons with varying ages are not easy to obtain. One of the skeletons from Carolina Biological Supply does show epiphyseal lines, and another is of a child with concomitant incomplete dentition; these are particularly useful for the subadult segments of this lab. The adult part of this lab typically requires the use of real human bone, or unusually good reproductions, because the inexpensive plastic skeletons do not have the detail necessary to do symphyseal surface, auricular surface, and so on.

**Exercise Worksheet 9.1: Estimating Age at Death (Subadults) Using Long Limb Bone Measurements**

Name: _____ Date: _____

Case/Accession number: _____

### Age Ranges From Long Limb Bone Lengths

Fem

Tib

Fib

Hum

Uln

Rad

| 3 | 4 | 5 | 6 | 7 | 8 | Br | 2 | 4 | 6 | 8 | 10 | 12 |

**Fetal age (in months)** **Age (in years)**

Age: _____

Comments: _____

_____

_____

_____

_____

## Exercise Worksheet 9.2: Estimating Age at Death (Subadults) Using Union of Primary Ossification Centers

Name: _____ Date: _____

Case/Accession number: _____

| Site | Time of Closure |
| --- | --- |
| *Fontanelles* | |
| Spheonoid and mastoid | Soon after birth |
| Posterior | During first year |
| Anterior | During second year |
| *Mandible* | |
| Right and left halves | Completed by second year |
| *Frontal* | |
| Right and left halves | In second year (remains open in as many as 10% of people) |
| *Atlas* | |
| Union of posterior halves | In third year |
| Union of anterior halves | In sixth year |
| *Axis* | |
| Dens, body, and both arches | In third and fourth years |
| *Occipital* | |
| Squamous with lateral parts | In fifth year |
| Lateral and basilar parts | In sixth year |

Taken from data in Stewart (1979).

Age: _____

Comments: _____

_____

_____

**Exercise Worksheet 9.3: Estimating Age at Death (Subadults) Using Tooth Formation and Eruption**

Name: _____   Date: _____

Case/Accession number: _____

## Tooth Calcification Stage

| | Br | 1 | 2 | 3 | 4 | 5 | 6 | 7 | 8 | 9 | 10 | 11 | 12 |
|---|---|---|---|---|---|---|---|---|---|---|---|---|---|
| dc | | | | | | | | | | | | | |
| $dm_1$ | | | | | | | | | | | | | |
| $dm_2$ | | | | | | | | | | | | | |
| $I^1$ | | | | | | | | | | | | | |
| $I^2$ | | | | | | | | | | | | | |
| $C^1$ | | | | | | | | | | | | | |
| $P^1$ | | | | | | | | | | | | | |
| $P^2$ | | | | | | | | | | | | | |
| $M^1$ | | | | | | | | | | | | | |
| $M^2$ | | | | | | | | | | | | | |
| $M^3$ | | | | | | | | | | | | | |
| $I_1$ | | | | | | | | | | | | | |
| $I_2$ | | | | | | | | | | | | | |
| $C_1$ | | | | | | | | | | | | | |
| $P_1$ | | | | | | | | | | | | | |
| $P_2$ | | | | | | | | | | | | | |
| $M_1$ | | | | | | | | | | | | | |
| $M_2$ | | | | | | | | | | | | | |
| $M_3$ | | | | | | | | | | | | | |

Age: _____          Age from tooth eruption: _____

Comments: _____

_____

_____

_____

**Exercise Worksheet 9.4: Estimating Age at Death (Subadults) Using Epiphyseal Union**

Name: _____     Date: _____

Case/Accession number: _____

| | Br | 5 | 10 | 15 | 20 | 25 | 30 |
|---|---|---|---|---|---|---|---|
| Spheno-occipital synchondrosis | | | | | | | |
| Clavicle (medial epiphysis) | | | | | | | |
| Sacrum (S1–S2) | | | | | | | |
| Sacrum (S2–S3) | | | | | | | |
| Sacrum (S3–S5) | | | | | | | |
| Radius (distal epiphysis) | | | | | | | |
| Femur (greater trochanter) | | | | | | | |
| Tibia (proximal epiphysis) | | | | | | | |
| Femur (head, lesser trochanter) | | | | | | | |
| Humerus (head) | | | | | | | |
| Scapula (acromion) | | | | | | | |
| Os coxae (iliac crest) | | | | | | | |
| Femur (distal epiphysis) | | | | | | | |
| Fibula (proximal epiphysis) | | | | | | | |
| Fibula (distal epiphysis) | | | | | | | |
| Tibia (distal epiphysis) | | | | | | | |
| Radius (proximal epiphysis) | | | | | | | |
| Humerus (medial epicondyle) | | | | | | | |
| Humerus (distal epiphysis) | | | | | | | |
| Vertebrae (neural arch-centrum) | | | | | | | |
| Vertebrae (right and left neural arch) | | | | | | | |
| Occipital (a) | | | | | | | |
| Occipital (b) | | | | | | | |

Age: _____

Comments: _____

_____

_____

_____

_____

# Exercise Worksheet 9.5: Estimating Age at Death (Adults) Using Symphyseal Surface

Name: _____   Date: _____

Case/Accession number: _____

## Changes in the Symphyseal Surface[1]

| Phase | Pubic Face | Borders | | Extremities | | Miscellaneous |
| --- | --- | --- | --- | --- | --- | --- |
| | | *Ventral* | *Dorsal* | *Upper* | *Lower* | |
| I | Ridges and furrows extending to the pubic tubercle | Beveling may have started | Undefined | Undefined | Undefined | Ossific nodules may be present |
| II | Ridges and furrows may be present | Rampart beginning to form | Undefined | Starting to be defined | Starting to be defined | Ossific nodules may present |
| III | Smooth or ridges and furrows still present | Rampart almost complete | Plateau complete | More defined | Lower almost defined | Ossific nodules may be fusing to form upper extremity and ventral border |
| IV | Fine grained with remnants of ridges and furrows (pubic tubercle distinct from face) | Defined but hiatus can occur in upper part | Defined with possible lipping | Defined | Defined | Oval outline complete, possibly with rim; ligamentous outgrowths may occur inferiorly |
| V | Slightly depressed compared to rim | Defined with possible breakdown superiorly | Defined with moderate lipping | Defined | Defined | Rim complete; ligamentous outgrowths more prominent |
| VI | Depression more common with pitting, porosity, and crenulations | Breaking down | Breaking down | Breaking down | Breaking down | Rim eroding; ligamentous outgrowths more prominent |

1  Summarized from Suchey and Katz (1998).

Sex: _____

Age: _____

Comments: _____
_____
_____

## Exercise Worksheet 9.6: Estimating Age at Death (Adults) Using Auricular Surface of the Os Coxae

Name: _____  Date: _____

Case/Accession number: _____

### Changes in the Auricular Surface by Age Range

| Age Range | Transverse Organization | Granularity | Apical Activity | Retroauricular Area | Porosity |
|---|---|---|---|---|---|
| 20–24 | Billowing | Very fine | None | None | None |
| 25–29 | Billows being replaced by striae | Slightly coarser | None | None | None |
| 30–34 | Less billowing more straie | Distinctly coarser | None | Slight, may be present | Some micro |
| 35–39 | Marked fewer billows and straie | Uniformly coarse | Slight activity | Slight | Slight micro |
| 40–44 | No billows; vague striae | Transition from granular to dense | Slight | Slight to moderate | Micro, may be macro |
| 45–49 | None | Dense bone | Slight to moderate | Moderate | Little or no macro |
| 50–60 | None (surface irregular) | Dense bone | Marked | Moderate to marked | Macro present |
| 60+ | None | Destruction of bone | Marked | Marked with osteophytes | Macro |

Summarized from data in Lovejoy et al. (1985).

Age: _____

Comments: _____

_____

_____

**Exercise Worksheet 9.7: Estimating Age at Death (Adults) Using Sternal Rib Ends**

Name: _____ Date: _____

Case/Accession number: _____

## Changes in the Sternal Rib Ends (White Males and Females)

| Age Range | Surface Bone | Surface Contour | Rim Edge | Rim Contour |
|---|---|---|---|---|
| 19 and under | Smooth | Flat/indented with billows | Rounded | Regular to slightly wavy |
| 20–29 | Smooth to porous | Indented; U- to V-shaped | Rounded | Wavy to irregular |
| 30–39 | More porous | V- to U-shaped | Sharp | Irregular |
| 40–49 | More porous | U-shaped with flaring | Sharp | Irregular with projections |
| 50–59 | Light and porous | U-shaped and deeper | Sharp | Irregular with projections |
| 60–69 | Light and porous | U-shaped and deeper | Sharp | Irregular with projections |
| 70+ | Deteriorating | U-shaped | Sharp with thin walls | Irregular with projections (some with windows) |

Condensed from data in İşcan et al. (1984, 1985).

Age: _____

Comments: _____

_____

_____

**Exercise Worksheet 9.8: Estimating Age at Death (Adults) Using Suture Closure**

Name: _____     Date: _____

Case/Accession number: _____

## Sites on the Ectocranium

| Site | Score | | |
|------|-------|---|---|
| | *Vault* | *Lateral-Anterior* | |
| Midlambdoid | | N/A | |
| Lambda | | N/A | |
| Obelion | | N/A | |
| Anterior-sagittal | | N/A | |
| Bregma | | N/A | |
| Midcoronal | | | |
| Pterion | N/A | | |
| Sphenofrontal | N/A | | |
| Inferior sphenotemporal | N/A | | |
| Superior sphenotemporal | N/A | | |
| Total | _____ | _____ | |
| Stage | _____ | _____ | |
| Age range | _____ | _____ | |

| | | | |
|---|---|---|---|
| **Age from endocranial suture closure:** | 20–34 | 35–49 | 50+ |
| **Age from palatal suture closure:** | 20–32 | 33–50 | Over 50 |

Age: _____

Comments: _____

_____

_____

# 10 Calculation of Stature

An estimation of stature is the final demographic characteristic in osteological analysis. Although rearticulating the skeleton and measuring the resultant length will provide an estimate of this parameter, this is much more difficult than it appears (e.g., the bones must be spaced the same as they are in life). Also, this requires all body segments that are part of height (i.e., skull, all vertebrae, pelvis, leg bones, foot bones) to be present, which is not common in forensic anthropology. Thus, formulae that allow for the estimation of stature from measurements of long limb bones comprise the most commonly used method for determining this parameter. These formulae can also be used with fragmented long limb bones because the relationship between bone segments and full bone length is known. In these cases, the process is to calculate the bone length from the fragment, and enter this length into a stature reconstruction formula. After the stature is calculated, adjustments due to age, bone shrinkage, and discrepancies between reported and measured height can be applied to increase the accuracy of the estimate.

## Learning Objectives

During this lab, you will learn how to take the measurements necessary to estimate the living stature of persons from their skeletal remains, using full bone lengths as well as bone fragments. You will use these measurements in various calculations to arrive at a stature estimate. Then, you will learn to apply adjustments to your computation to account for various factors that affect stature.

## Expected Outcomes

By the end of this lab, you should able to:

- Calculate living height of individuals by using measurements of their long limb bones.
- Calculate living height using fragmented long limb bones.
- Calculate living height from body segments involved in height (e.g., skull, vertebrae, lower limb bones, and ankle bones).
- Make adjustments to your calculation due to bone shrinkage, age, and reporting error.

## Minimum Materials

Any of the long limb bones (femur, tibia, fibula, humerus, radius, ulna)
Bone board

## Optional Materials

Sliding caliper
Spreading caliper
Skeleton with skull, full vertebral column (including sacrum), femur, tibia, talus, and calcaneous
Fragmentary femur, tibia, humerus, or radius

**Exercise 10.1: Calculating Stature Using Long Limb Bones**

The most common method for estimating stature is to use regression formulae to calculate living height from measurements of the long limb bones (i.e., those bones of the arms and legs, minus the hands and feet). Read the section Regression Equations in Chapter 1 as well as the section Long Limb Bones of Chapter 10 of the textbook. Now, using a bone board as pictured in Figure 1.6 of the textbook (sometimes long sliding calipers can be used for the radius and ulna) and referring to the appropriate figures in this manual, measure the maximum length of the humerus (see Figure 10.1 of this manual), ulna (see Figure 10.2), and radius (see Figure 10.3), as well as the fibula (see Figure 10.4) and femur (see Figure 10.5). The length of the tibia is more complex in that it requires that the distance be taken from the midpoint of the proximal surface of the lateral condyle to the tip of the malleolus (see Figure 10.6). All of the bone lengths can be increased by 1.5% (i.e., multiplied by 1.015) if the osteological material has undergone noticeable drying.

Once taken, these dimensions can be entered on Exercise Worksheet 10.1 along with the coefficients of the appropriate stature reconstruction formulae presented in Table 10.1 of this manual. As you can see, these equations are presented for White and Black males and females, but only Asian and Hispanic males. If the lab skeleton is an Asian or a Hispanic female, use the male formulae for the appropriate ancestral group, and multiply the result by 0.92 (the proportion that women are of male size) to arrive at a stature approximation. Ask your instructor for the ancestral group and sex of the laboratory bones before making any of the calculations. Each measurement is multiplied first by its coefficient, and then added to the intercept value to arrive at an estimate of living height. (These values are in centimeters; to convert them to inches and feet as used by law enforcement agencies, see Box 10.1 or Chapter 1 of this manual.)

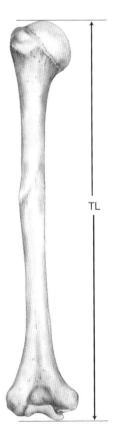

*Figure 10.1* Total length (TL) of the humerus.

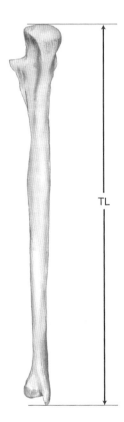

*Figure 10.2* Total length (TL) of the ulna.

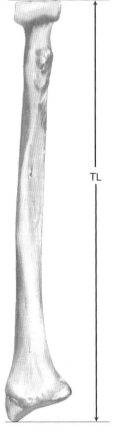

*Figure 10.3* Total length (TL) of the radius.

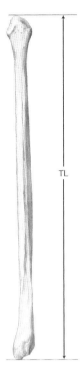

*Figure 10.4* Total length (TL) of the fibula.

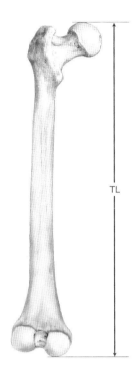

*Figure 10.5* Total length (TL) of the femur.

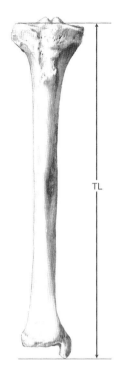

*Figure 10.6* Total length (TL) of the tibia.

*Table 10.1* Stature Reconstruction Formulas Using Long Limb Bones, Separated by Ancestral Group and Sex[1]

| Formula | SE | Formula | SE |
|---|---|---|---|
| **White Males** | | **Black Males** | |
| St = 3.574 × Hum + 57.21 | 5.71 | St = 3.277 × Hum + 65.46 | 5.72 |
| St = 4.525 × Rad + 61.22 | 5.70 | St = 4.235 × Rad + 63.46 | 5.07 |
| St = 4.534 × Uln + 53.33 | 5.66 | St = 3.979 × Uln + 62.95 | 5.79 |
| St = 2.701 × Fem + 48.10 | 5.12 | St = 2.455 × Fem + 56.66 | 4.84 |
| St = 2.981 × Tib + 62.95 | 5.06 | St = 2.455 × Tib + 75.48 | 5.03 |
| St = 2.832 × Fib + 66.96 | 5.15 | St = 2.665 × Fib + 69.39 | 4.53 |
| St = 1.728 × (Hum + Fem) + 36.76 | 5.16 | St = 1.522 × (Hum + Fem) + 50.69 | 4.83 |
| St = 1.525 × (Fem + Tib) + 44.19 | 4.81 | St = 1.295 × (Fem + Tib) + 60.18 | 4.73 |
| St = 1.556 × (Fem + Fib) + 42.77 | 4.90 | St = 1.341 × (Fem + Fib) + 57.18 | 4.28 |
| **White Females** | | **Black Females** | |
| St = 2.534 × Hum + 86.62 | 5.32 | St = 3.785 × Hum + 47.35 | 4.56 |
| St = 3.530 × Rad + 83.29 | 4.81 | St = 3.781 × Rad + 75.20 | 5.01 |
| St = 3.346 × Uln + 82.82 | 4.51 | St = 3.285 × Uln + 80.70 | 4.18 |
| St = 2.624 × Fem + 49.26 | 3.58 | St = 2.449 × Fem + 54.86 | 4.34 |
| St = 2.351 × Tib + 80.11 | 4.26 | St = 2.855 × Tib + 58.20 | 3.83 |
| St = 2.487 × Fib + 76.51 | 4.16 | St = 2.993 × Fib + 55.83 | 4.29 |
| St = 1.656 × (Hum + Fem) + 46.71 | 3.72 | St = 1.566 × (Hum + Fem) + 46.12 | 4.12 |
| St = 1.330 × (Fem + Tib) + 58.37 | 4.01 | St = 1.340 × (Fem + Tib) + 54.75 | 3.50 |
| St = 1.382 × (Fem + Fib) + 54.89 | 3.85 | St = 1.365 × (Fem + Fib) + 54.28 | 3.87 |
| **Asian Males** | | **Hispanic Males** | |
| St = 2.68 × Hum + 83.19 | 4.25 | St = 2.92 × Hum + 73.94 | 4.24 |
| St = 3.54 × Rad + 82.00 | 4.60 | St = 3.55 × Rad + 80.71 | 4.04 |
| St = 3.48 × Uln + 77.45 | 4.66 | St = 3.56 × Uln + 74.56 | 4.05 |
| St = 2.15 × Fem + 72.57 | 3.80 | St = 2.44 × Fem + 58.67 | 2.99 |
| St = 2.40 × Fib + 80.56 | 3.24 | St = 2.50 × Fib + 75.44 | 3.52 |

[1] Data for White and Black males and females are from Table 2 of Wilson et al. (2010); data for Asian and Hispanic males taken from Trotter (1970).

---

**Box 10.1   Conversion of Metric Measure to Inches and Feet**

To convert metric measurements to inches and feet, you can either use the appropriate button on your calculator or perform the following steps:

1. Divide the formula result by 2.54 to get inches.
2. Divide the result of Step 1 by 12 to get feet.
3. Multiply the digits to the right of the decimal point from the result of Step 2 by 1.2 to get inches.
4. Stature, in feet and inches, is the digits to the left of the decimal point from Step 2 (feet) and the result from Step 3 (inches).

---

## Exercise 10.2: Calculating Stature Using the Fully Method

To use the Fully Method to estimate height, measurements of a number of body segments must be taken: skull height, the heights of the vertebrae, the lengths of the femur and tibia, and the ankle height. First, measure the skull height by determining the distance from basion to bregma using a spreading caliper (see Figure 10.7). Next, measure the vertebral heights from the superior to the inferior surfaces of the bodies (see Figure 10.8); do not measure the atlas but do measure the height of the first segment of the sacrum. Next, measure the bicondylar length of the femur (Figure 10.9); this involves ensuring that both condyles rest against the vertical part of the bone board before the sliding part contacts the femoral head. Then, measure the length of the tibia (Figure 10.6). Finally, measure the ankle height by determining the distance from the superior surface of the talus to the inferior surface of the calcaneous when they are held in natural articulation (Figure 10.10). Again, all of the bone lengths taken can be increased by 1.5% (i.e., multiplied by 1.015) if the osteological material has undergone noticeable drying.

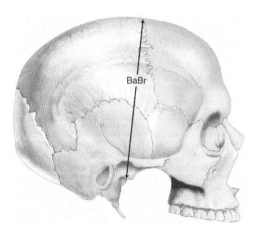

*Figure 10.8* Thickness (T) of the vertebral body.

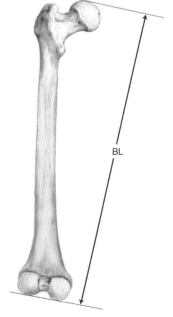

*Figure 10.7* Basion to bregma (BaBr) height of skull.

*Figure 10.9* Bicondylar length (BL) of the femur.

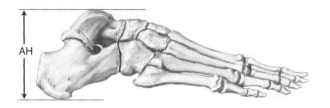

*Figure 10.10* Ankle height (AH) from the talus and calcaneous.

As these measurements are taken, enter them into the appropriate spaces on Exercise Worksheet 10.2. Once completed, these values can be summed down the columns and then added across the bottom. The final step in getting an estimate of stature using the Fully Method is the addition of the appropriate correction factor for soft tissue from Table 10.2 in this manual. (Again, these values are in centimeters; to convert them to inches and feet as used by law enforcement agencies, see Box 10.1 in this manual.) If the Raxter and colleagues method is being used, enter the total bone sum into the appropriate formula.

## Exercise 10.3: Calculating Stature From Fleshed Body Segments

As discussed in the textbook, forensic anthropologists often are involved in the identification of fleshed body segments of victims of mass disasters such as airplane crashes, terrorist attacks, and even genocide. In this exercise, fellow classmates will represent victims of one of these incidents so that you can determine their stature from various body segments. In addition, you can measure their stature directly to compare your estimate with the real amount. If only a measuring tape is available, then only the first two measurements listed in Table 10.3 in this manual can be taken; if the lab has an anthropometer rod, then all dimensions can be performed. Follow the directions in Table 10.3 for obtaining each measurement, and using the formulae from Table 10.4, calculate the stature of your "victim" on Exercise Worksheet 10.3.

*Table 10.2* Soft Tissue Correction Factors for the Fully Method (in Centimeters)

| Calculated Height | Male | Female |
|---|---|---|
| 153.5 cm or less | 12.2 | 11.2 |
| Over 153.5 cm and less than 165.4 cm | 12.8 | 11.8 |
| 165.5 cm or above | 14.0 | 12.9 |

Male data from Fully quoted by Stewart (1979), adjusted with information in Raxter et al. (2006); female values 92% of male values.

*Table 10.3* Measurement Definitions on Fleshed Bodies[1]

| Measurement | Definition |
|---|---|
| UPARMLTH | Taken with the right arm flexed 90° at the elbow and the palm facing up. On the right scapula, locate and *mark with a horizontal line* the uppermost edge of the posterior border of the acromion process. Hold the zero end of the measuring tape at this mark and extend the tape down the posterior surface of the arm to the tip of the olecranon process (the bony part of the mid-elbow). |
| UPLEGLTH | Taken with the upper leg at right angles to the body, and the knee bent at 90°. Position the small sliding caliper as if you were measuring the breadth of the patella. Position the caliper blades against the distal end of the femur on either side of the patella. The horizontal bar of the caliper should be touching, or close to the anterior surface of the thigh, proximal to the patella. Using the superior edge of the horizontal bar of the caliper as a guide, mark a line with a wax-based cosmetic pencil on the anterior surface of the thigh. Place the zero end of the steel measuring tape at the inguinal crease, just below the anterior superior iliac spine (this is easily located if the hips are in a sitting position). Do not apply pressure at the inguinal crease. . . . Extend the tape down the anterior midline of the thigh to the mark that was previously made proximal to the patella. |
| BUTTKLTH | The horizontal distance between the most posterior point on the buttock and the anterior point of the knee measured while the knee is flexed 90°. Measured along the lateral thigh with an anthropometer rod. |
| FOOTLGTH | The maximum length of the foot from the heel to the tip of the longest toe, measured with calipers. |
| FORHDLG | The horizontal distance between the posterior surface of the elbow and the tip of the middle finger taken while the elbow is flexed 90°. Measured with a caliper. |

*(Continued)*

*Table 10.3* (Continued)

| | |
|---|---|
| HANDLGTH | The distance from the tip of the styloid process of the radius to the tip of the middle finger. Measured with a caliper. |
| KNEEHTSI | The vertical distance between the bottom of the foot and the suprapatellar landmark (point on the superior surface of the patella when standing). Measured with an anthropometer rod with the knee flexed 90°. |
| LATFEMEP | The vertical distance between the bottom of the foot and the lateral femoral epicondyle. Measured with an anthropometer rod and lower leg in vertical position. |
| SHOUELLT | The distance between the superior tip of the acromial process of the scapula and the bottom of the elbow. Measured with a caliper with the upper arm vertical and the elbow flexed 90°. |
| SPAN | The distance between the tips of the middle fingers when the arms are horizontally outstretched. |

[1] UPARMLTH and UPLEGLTH are taken from Anthropometry and Physical Activity Monitor Procedures Manual of the National Health and Nutrition Examination Survey; all others taken from Gordon et al. (1989).

*Table 10.4* Stature Reconstruction Formulae Using Fleshed Body Segments[1]

| Group | Formula | SE |
|---|---|---|
| All | St = 61.27 × 2.88 (UPARMLTH) | 6.04 |
| Male | St = 83.25 × 2.38 (UPARMLTH) | 5.56 |
| Female | St = 88.8 × 2.05 (UPARMLTH) | 5.2 |
| White | St = 65.68 × 2.81 (UPARMLTH) | 5.84 |
| Black | St = 66.84 × 2.72 (UPARMLTH) | 6.36 |
| Hispanic | St = 60.26 × 2.87 (UPARMLTH) | 5.53 |
| White male | St = 95.87 × 2.1 (UPARMLTH) | 5.3 |
| White female | St = 97.02 × 1.88 (UPARMLTH) | 4.91 |
| Black male | St = 98.48 × 2 (UPARMLTH) | 5.34 |
| Black female | St = 100.65 × 1.72 (UPARMLTH) | 5.01 |
| Hispanic male | St = 83.71 × 2.31 (UPARMLTH) | 5.13 |
| Hispanic female | St = 84.91 × 2.11 (UPARMLTH) | 4.74 |
| All | St = 85.56 × 2.02 (UPLEGLTH) | 6.51 |
| Male | St = 103.77 × 1.67 (UPLEGLTH) | 5.77 |
| Female | St = 109.85 × 1.34 (UPLEGLTH) | 5.45 |
| White | St = 86.03 × 2.05 (UPLEGLTH) | 6.37 |
| Black | St = 84.18 × 2.02 (UPLEGLTH) | 6.58 |
| Hispanic | St = 87.74 × 1.94 (UPLEGLTH) | 6.04 |
| White male | St = 115.26 × 1.45 (UPLEGLTH) | 5.55 |
| White female | St = 114.02 × 1.28 (UPLEGLTH) | 5.19 |
| Black male | St = 105.83 × 1.61 (UPLEGLTH) | 5.35 |
| Black female | St = 118.24 × 1.11 (UPLEGLTH) | 5.26 |
| Hispanic male | St = 105.58 × 1.57 (UPLEGLTH) | 5.41 |
| Hispanic female | St = 109.88 × 1.28 (UPLEGLTH) | 5.03 |

[1] Taken from Adams and Herrmann (2009); measurement in millimeters, stature in centimeters.

*Table 10.5* Stature Reconstruction Formulae Using Fleshed Body Segments[1]

| Formula | SE | Formula | SE |
|---|---|---|---|
| *Males* | | *Females* | |
| St = 1.80 × BUTTKLTH + 64.94 | 3.99 | St = 1.60 × BUTTKLTH + 68.91 | 4.25 |
| St = 3.57 × FOOTLGTH + 79.24 | 4.77 | St = 3.50 × FOOTLGTH + 77.40 | 4.71 |
| St = 2.15 × FORHDLG + 71.70 | 4.43 | St = 1.94 × FORHDLG + 77.14 | 4.47 |
| St = 4.44 × HANDLGTH + 89.58 | 5.08 | St = 4.18 × HANDLGTH + 87.58 | 4.91 |
| St = 2.12 × KNEEHTSI + 57.17 | 3.11 | St = 2.07 × KNEEHTSI + 56.23 | 3.28 |
| St = 2.21 × LATFEMEP + 64.69 | 3.30 | St = 2.18 × LATFEMEP + 62.36 | 3.37 |
| St = 3.05 × SHOUELLT + 63.10 | 3.84 | St = 2.92 × SHOUELLT + 64.97 | 3.83 |
| St = 0.66 × SPAN + 54.45 | 3.37 | St = 0.62 × SPAN + 59.92 | 3.92 |

[1] Taken from Adams and Herrmann (2009); measurements in millimeters, stature in centimeters.

## Exercise 10.4: Calculating Stature Using Partial Long Limb Bones

To estimate stature from fragmented bones, use the information provided in Figure 10.11 and Table 10.9 of the textbook to determine which components of the laboratory fragmented long limb bone you can measure. Make the longest measurement possible from the fragment that you have (e.g., if you have the proximal tibia with points 1 through 4, do not measure only from points 1 to 3). Next, use the information in Table 10.11 of the textbook to determine the total length of the bone before breakage. For example, if a fragmentary male humerus has segment 1–2 that measures 3.2 centimeters long, and segment 2–3 is 25.0 centimeters long, the total length would be calculated as:

$$\text{Humeral segment} = (3.2 + 25.0) \times 100 \div (11.29 + 77.51) = 31.8 \tag{1}$$

Use Exercise Worksheet 10.3 for these calculations on the lab's bone fragment. When finished, enter the total bone length into the space provided along with the coefficients of the appropriate stature reconstruction formulae presented in Table 10.1 of this manual. Then calculate the stature.

## Exercise 10.5: Adjustments to Stature Calculations

As discussed in the textbook, several adjustments to stature can be made if the age and sex of the deceased is known so that your calculation of height more closely approximates the reported height on driver's licenses, and loss of stature through time. If the age of the decedent is known, use the information in Table 10.6 in this manual to subtract the average amount of statural decrease for the person's age group. Complete the section Adjustments to Stature on Exercise Worksheets 1, 2, and 4 by first entering the calculated stature and then subtracting the appropriate age factor. Similarly, if the sex is male, add 12 millimeters (1/2 inch) to the calculated stature to correct for errors in reported height; add 6 millimeters (1/4 inch) if the decedent is female. Again, enter the calculated height, and then add the adjustment for reported stature in the space provided on the worksheet. Thus, you will have three estimates of stature: calculated stature, stature adjusted (downward) for age, and stature adjusted (upward) for reporting error.

### NOTE TO INSTRUCTORS

This lab may require that you construct your own bone board for students to measure the long limb bones (the most commonly used method for calculating stature). These are not difficult to make; the shop at your institution should be able to create several of these for you in a short period of time for minimal cost. These do not have to be "works of art" to be effective; I constructed one of plywood and a wooden meter stick over 25 years ago, and although somewhat the worse for wear, it is as useable today as it was over a quarter of a century ago when it was made. Notice this chapter did not include determining stature from metacarpals, metatarsals, or vertebral column. I felt it would make this lab unnecessarily long. If you have a desire to estimate stature from these bones, you can use Exercise Worksheet 10.1 as a template by simply "whiting out" the names of the long limb bones, and substituting the names of the bones you are having the students measure. If you choose to do the Fully Method, consult Raxter et al. (2006) for information on the nuances of the measurements used in this technique.

When determining stature from fleshed body segments using students as specimens, it is not necessary to mark the person's body as indicated in some of the measurement definitions. Also, be cognizant of a student's feelings about being touched/measured by other students as some of these measurements are very invasive (e.g., UPLEGLTH, BUTTKLTH).

*Table 10.6* Average Amount of Decrease in Stature (in Millimeters) by Age Group for Males and Females

| Age Category | Males | Females |
|---|---|---|
| 46–49 | 3.1 | 0.1 |
| 50–59 | 7.2 | 2.8 |
| 60–69 | 16.0 | 12.5 |
| 70+ | 32.3 | 33.9 |

Summarized from data in Giles (1991).

## Exercise Worksheet 10.1: Calculating Stature Using Long Limb Bones

Name: _____    Date: _____

Case/Accession number: _____

*Note:* Be sure to multiply the bone length by the coefficient before adding the intercept.

### Calculation of Stature

| | | | | | | | | |
|---|---|---|---|---|---|---|---|---|
| Humerus length: | _____ | × | _____ (coefficient) | + | _____ (intercept) | = | _____ (stature) | |
| Radius length: | _____ | × | _____ (coefficient) | + | _____ (intercept) | = | _____ (stature) | |
| Ulna length: | _____ | × | _____ (coefficient) | + | _____ (intercept) | = | _____ (stature) | |
| Femur length: | _____ | × | _____ (coefficient) | + | _____ (intercept) | = | _____ (stature) | |
| Tibia length: | _____ | × | _____ (coefficient) | + | _____ (intercept) | = | _____ (stature) | |
| Fibula length: | _____ | × | _____ (coefficient) | + | _____ (intercept) | = | _____ (stature) | |

### Adjustments to Stature

*Adjustments for Age*
Calculated stature from:

| | | | | | |
|---|---|---|---|---|---|
| Humerus: | _____ | − | _____ (age adj.) | = | (stature) |
| Radius: | _____ | − | _____ (age adj.) | = | (stature) |
| Ulna: | _____ | − | _____ (age adj.) | = | (stature) |
| Femur: | _____ | − | _____ (age adj.) | = | (stature) |
| Tibia: | _____ | − | _____ (age adj.) | = | (stature) |
| Fibula: | _____ | − | _____ (age adj.) | = | (stature) |

*Adjustments for Reporting Error*
Calculated stature from:

| | | | | | |
|---|---|---|---|---|---|
| Humerus: | _____ | + | _____ <br> (reporting error) | = | _____ <br> (stature) |
| Radius: | _____ | + | _____ <br> (reporting error) | = | _____ <br> (stature) |
| Ulna: | _____ | + | _____ <br> (reporting error) | = | _____ <br> (stature) |
| Femur: | _____ | + | _____ <br> (reporting error) | = | _____ <br> (stature) |
| Tibia: | _____ | + | _____ <br> (reporting error) | = | _____ <br> (stature) |
| Fibula: | _____ | + | _____ <br> (reporting error) | = | _____ <br> (stature) |

**Comments:** _____

_____

_____

_____

## Exercise Worksheet 10.2: Calculating Stature Using the Fully Method

Name: _____ Date: _____

Case/Accession number: _____

Basion–bregma: _____

| | Cervical | Thoracic | | Lumbar |
|---|---|---|---|---|
| | | *Height of Vertebral Bodies* | | |
| C2: | _____ | T1: _____ | L1: | _____ |
| C3: | _____ | T2: _____ | L2: | _____ |
| C4: | _____ | T3: _____ | L3: | _____ |
| C5: | _____ | T4: _____ | L4: | _____ |
| C6: | _____ | T5: _____ | L5: | _____ |
| C7: | _____ | T6: _____ | | |
| | | T7: _____ | | |
| S1: | _____ | T8: _____ | | |
| Femur: | _____ | T9: _____ | | |
| Tibia: | _____ | T10: _____ | | |
| | | T11: _____ | | |
| Ankle: | _____ | T12: _____ | | |

Total: _____ + _____ + _____ + _____ = _____
(soft tissue correction)

$11.7 + .996 \times$ _____ = _____
(Sum of all bones)

$12.1 + 1.009 \times$ _____ $- 0.0426 \times$ _____ = _____
(Sum of all bones)     (age)

**Adjustments to Stature**

*Adjustment for Age*

Stature: _____ − _____ = _____
(age adj.)          (stature)

*Adjustment for Reporting Error*

Stature: _____ + _____ = _____
       (reporting error)          (stature)

**Comments:** _____

_____

_____

_____

**Exercise Worksheet 10.3: Calculating Stature From Fleshed Body Segments**

Name: _____ Date: _____

Case/Accession number: _____

*Note:* Be sure to multiply the bone length by the coefficient before adding the intercept.

**Calculation of Stature**

UPARMLTH: _____ × _____ + _____ = _____
                  (coefficient)      (intercept)      (stature)

UPLEGLTH: _____ × _____ + _____ = _____
                  (coefficient)      (intercept)      (stature)

BUTTKLTH: _____ × _____ + _____ = _____
                  (coefficient)      (intercept)      (stature)

FOOTLGTH: _____ × _____ + _____ = _____
                  (coefficient)      (intercept)      (stature)

FORHDLG: _____ × _____ + _____ = _____
                  (coefficient)      (intercept)      (stature)

HANDLGTH: _____ × _____ + _____ = _____
                  (coefficient)      (intercept)      (stature)

KNEEHTSI: _____ × _____ + _____ = _____
                  (coefficient)      (intercept)      (stature)

LATFEMEP: _____ × _____ + _____ = _____
                  (coefficient)      (intercept)      (stature)

SHOUELLT: _____ × _____ + _____ = _____
                  (coefficient)      (intercept)      (stature)

SPAN: _____ × _____ + _____ = _____
                  (coefficient)      (intercept)      (stature)

**Stature:** _____

**Comments:** _____

_____

_____

**Exercise Worksheet 10.4: Calculating Stature Using Partial Long Limb Bones**

Name: _____ Date: _____

Case/Accession number: _____

Femoral segment: _____ × 100 ÷ _____ = _____
                                        (% of segments)        (length)

Femur length: _____ × _____ + _____ = _____
                                  (coefficient)       (intercept)        (stature)

Tibial segment: _____ × 100 ÷ _____ = _____
                                       (% of segments)       (length)

Tibial length: _____ × _____ + _____ = _____
                                  (coefficient)       (intercept)        (stature)

Humeral segment: _____ × 100 ÷ _____ = _____
                                        (% of segments)       (length)

Humeral length: _____ × _____ + _____ = _____
                                   (coefficient)       (intercept)        (stature)

Radial segment: _____ × 100 ÷ _____ = _____
                                       (% of segments)       (length)

Radius length: _____ × _____ + _____ = _____
                                  (coefficient)       (intercept)        (stature)

*Adjustments to Stature Calculations*

*Adjustments for Age*

Calculated stature from:

Femur: _____ − _____ = _____
                            (age adj.)          (stature)

Tibia: _____ − _____ = _____
                            (age adj.)          (stature)

Humerus: _____ − _____ = _____
                              (age adj.)          (stature)

Radius: _____ − _____ = _____
                             (age adj.)          (stature)

*Adjustments for Reporting Error*

Calculated stature from:

Femur: _____ + _____ = _____
                                    (reporting error)            (stature)

Tibia: _____ + _____ = _____
                                    (reporting error)            (stature)

Humerus: _____ + _____ = _____
                                    (reporting error)            (stature)

Radius: _____ + _____ = _____
                                    (reporting error)            (stature)

**Comments:** _____

_____

_____

_____

# 11 Death, Trauma, and the Skeleton

As described in the textbook, forensic anthropology involves providing information concerning cause and manner of death. From skeletal remains, the only source of data on these two issues involves trauma to bone. Thus, forensic anthropologists must be knowledgeable of the characteristics of trauma on human bone to be able to provide law enforcement information relating to these two factors.

## Learning Objectives

The purpose of this lab is to acquaint you with the different expressions of trauma in human bone. Also explored are the different forces that cause trauma, and three of the four types of trauma that can occur—projectile, blunt, and sharp—plus a miscellaneous category. Finally, characteristics of bone injuries that help identify trauma in relation to death (i.e., before, around, or after) will be studied.

## Expected Outcomes

By the end of this lab, you should be able to:

- Recognize the basics of bone trauma, including distinguishing fractures from infractions, simple from comminuted, and radiating from hoop fractures.
- Recognize characteristics of the forces that cause bone trauma.
- Recognize three types of trauma: blunt, sharp, and projectile. (Miscellaneous will not be explored.)
- Recognize the characteristics that distinguish antemortem, perimortem, and postmortem breaks.

## Minimum Materials

Picture of a human bone or structure (e.g., skull) with traumatic injury, preferably multiple views

## Optional Materials

Human bone (plastic or real) or structure (e.g., skull) with traumatic injury

## Exercise 11.1: Basics of Bone Trauma

Before commencing this lab, read the section Basics of Bone Trauma in Chapter 11 of the textbook. As described in that section, trauma to bone can cause a discontinuity (i.e., break) when enough force is applied. If this discontinuity travels completely through the bone, it is called a fracture (see Figure 11.1 in this manual), while it is an infraction when the fracture is incomplete (Figure 11.2 in this manual). Also, there are two types of discontinuities recognized here: displacements and lines. Displacement refers to breaks where surfaces that once were continuous no longer meet, or meet at an unnatural angle (e.g., hinge fractures, green stick fractures). When a single bone is broken into two segments, it is referred to as a simple fracture (Figure 11.1a in this manual), whereas comminuted fracture refers to a break that results in multiple fragments of bone (Figure 11.1b in this manual). Fracture lines are discontinuities that can take two forms. When they originate near the point of impact and spread outward, they are called radiating lines. When they encircle the point of impact, they are called concentric or hoop fractures (Figure 11.3 in this manual).

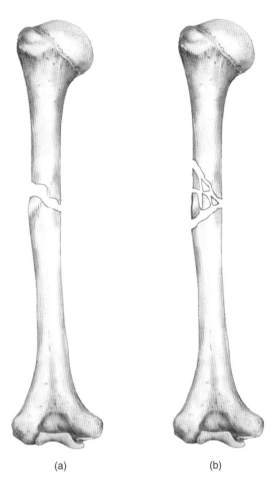

(a)          (b)

*Figure 11.1* Examples of complete fractures: (a) simple; (b) comminuted (with multiple fragmentation of bone).

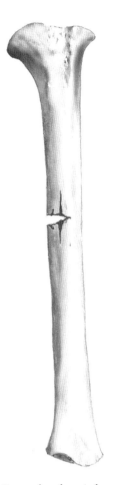

*Figure 11.2* Example of an infraction: a green stick fracture of the tibia.

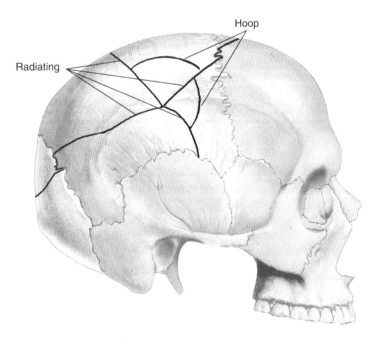

*Figure 11.3* Two types of fracture lines in the skull: radiating and hoop (concentric).

Finally, bone that is whole, yet appears to be collapsed, may indicate a stress or fatigue fracture that occurred over a long period of time.

Now, observe the lab bone for the characteristics of breaks described here. Does the bone show a complete or incomplete fracture? If the fracture is complete, is the bone separated into two (simple fracture) or multiple parts (comminuted fracture)? Are there fracture lines, and if so, do they radiate from a single area that appears to be the point of impact (radiating fracture), or do they surround that area (hoop fracture)? Finally, is the bone whole, but with a collapsed look? Now, complete the Exercise 11.1 section of the exercise worksheet. Describe the break seen in the lab bone in as much detail as possible. Be sure to distinguish between simple and comminuted breaks, displacements and fracture lines, and radiating from hoop fractures.

## Exercise 11.2: Forces Causing Trauma

Before starting this exercise, familiarize yourself with the section Characteristics of Forces Causing Trauma in Chapter 11 in the textbook. As described there, three characteristics of forces that cause bone injury need to be understood: direction, speed, and focus. Five directions of force are recognized: tension, compression, torsion, bending, and shearing (see Figure 11.4 of this manual). Tension is a force that pulls on bone, usually along its long axis, that results most often in displacement of a bony process (such as a tubercle) at the attachment site of a tendon. Compression forces push down on bone causing complete or incomplete fractures with (sometimes) numerous fracture lines radiating from the point of impact. Torsion forces are those that cause a twisting action on a bone. The resultant fracture often spirals down the long axis of a bone. Bending forces impact the side of a structure at approximately right angles to its long axis and cause a break through its cross section. A common type of this injury is the parry fracture of the ulna caused when victims raise their forearms in a position of self-defense, to ward off a blow. Finally, shearing forces result when one segment of the bone is immobilized while force is applied to a different segment. The Colles's fracture of the distal radius is a common example of this type of injury.

The next factor to consider is the speed of the force: dynamic or static. Dynamic force refers to sudden stress that is delivered powerfully and at high speed. Most of the fractures described earlier are caused by dynamic forces. By contrast, static force is stress that is applied slowly, starting at low strength and building to the point where the bone breaks. Although all of the fractures described in this chapter can result from this type of force, it is rarely the cause of bone displacements. Finally, consider the focus of the trauma-causing force. Narrow focus means that the force is applied to a single point or a thin line, while wide focus indicates that the force was delivered over a large area of bone.

Now, observe the lab bone for the characteristics described earlier. Is there evidence of a tension force applied to the bone (e.g., a process that has broken off)? Are there fracture lines radiating from a point of impact, indicating compression force? Do the break surfaces spiral down around the bone? Does the force appear to have impacted the side of the bone, with or without one of the segments held stationary? After making these observations, fill out the Exercise 11.2 section of the exercise worksheet. Be careful when you identify the type of force causing the break; distinguishing between some types (e.g., bending versus shearing) is not as easy as it appears. Also, justify your reasoning.

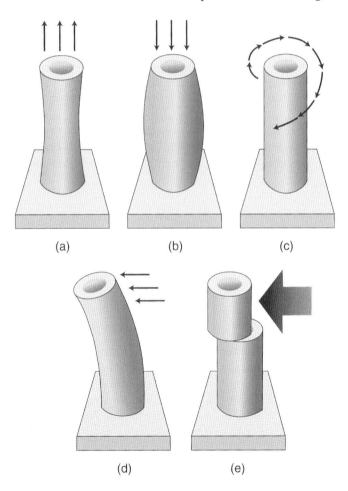

*Figure 11.4* The five directions of force that can cause bone fractures: (a) tension; (b) compression; (c) torsion; (d) bending; (e) shearing.

## Exercise 11.3: Types of Trauma

Before commencing this part of the lab, read the section Types of Trauma in the textbook. As described there, forensic anthropologists recognize four types of trauma: blunt, sharp, projectile, and miscellaneous. Blunt force trauma refers to any injury caused by compression, bending, and (occasionally) shearing forces, which is applied dynamically over a wide focus. Discontinuities and fracture lines are common and wounds can be both simple or comminuted fractures. Sharp trauma results when compression or shearing forces are applied dynamically over a narrow focus. This type of trauma can appear as punctures, chop marks, or incisions. Projectile trauma results when a bullet, arrow, or other airborne object impacts a bone with compressive or bending force that is applied dynamically over a small area. This can result in simple or comminuted fracture with multiple fracture lines. Finally, there are a variety of miscellaneous forces such as static pressure, generalized dynamic pressures, sawing, chemical, and heat.

Now, observe the lab bone for the characteristics described earlier. Is the point of impact small or large? Does it appear to have been caused by a projectile or some other object? Are there fracture lines near the point of impact? Surrounding the point of impact? Is the bone shattered into several fragments? Now, fill out the Exercise 11.3 section of the exercise worksheet by circling the type of injury seen in the lab bone. Justify your answer in the space provided; this is important because (as with other topics in this lab) distinguishing between the different types of trauma is not as easy as it appears.

## Exercise 11.4: Timing of Bone Injury

Familiarize yourself with the section Timing of Bone Injury in the textbook. In forensics, three timings (in relation to death) are recognized: antemortem, perimortem, and postmortem. Antemortem trauma refers to trauma that occurred before death, such that there is partial or complete healing. Characteristics of this timing of injury include porosity (pores near the breaks that indicates bone activity and resorption), rounding of the edges of the break, and callus formation. This latter structure starts first with fibrous bone extending across the break, which is eventually replaced by lamellar bone. The callus is irregular in shape, has a disorganized surface, and is raised above the surrounding area. By contrast, perimortem injuries always have sharp edges, indicative of an injury without healing. In addition, perimortem injuries can show hinging (bent sections of a bone), fracture lines (which would have healed in antemortem trauma), angled or jagged break surfaces, and (in some cases) staining from a hematoma. The last type of injury is postmortem damage. These are breaks that usually do not exhibit radiating fracture lines, have break surfaces at right angles to the long axis of a bone, almost flat break surfaces, and lighter color on the break surface than on the rest of the bone.

Now, observe the lab bones for the characteristics described in this section. Is the bone in two or more pieces? If it is broken, are the edges of the break sharp or dull? Are there fracture lines; and, if so, are their edges sharp or rounded? Is there porosity near the break? Is there a raised area with a disorganized surface over the break? If the bone is in two or more pieces, is the surface of the break jagged or flat? Does the break surface form a right (90°) angle with the long axis of the bone, or does it slant across the axis? Finally, is the surface of the break white or off-white, particularly in comparison to the rest of the bone? After making these observations, complete the last section of the exercise worksheet. Be sure to justify your judgment as to the timing of the injury seen in the lab bone.

### *NOTE TO INSTRUCTORS*

This, and the following chapters on trauma analysis, will require access to skeletons, casts, or good photos that show the types of trauma being studied. I was lucky to have access to the vast osteological collection at the University of New Mexico; however, there are only three or four such collections in the entire country. Thus, you probably will have to rely on casts to illustrate skeletal trauma. Luckily, there has been a marked improvement in the availability of such casts since the first edition of this manual appeared. A number are now available from places like Bone Clones and France Casting that should meet your needs. If your institution lacks resources to purchase these casts, photos of skeletons with various types of trauma can be found on various forensic anthropology websites. By asking permission for their use, you should be able to get enough examples of the various traumata for a lab session.

Notice that there are two copies of the exercise worksheet. These are provided to allow students to complete multiple copies of these sheets if your lab has a good collection of bones exhibiting trauma.

**Exercise Worksheets 11.1 Through 11.4: Trauma Analysis (Copy 1)**

Name: _____ Date: _____

Case/Accession number: _____

*Exercise 11.1 Basics of Bone Trauma*

Description: _____
_____
_____
_____
_____

*Exercise 11.2 Forces Causing Trauma*

Direction of force (circle one):

Tension                Compression                Torsion

Bending                Shearing                   Other: _____

Justification: _____
_____
_____

Speed of force (circle one):     Dynamic        Static
Justification: _____
_____
_____

Focus of force (circle one):     Narrow        Wide
Justification: _____
_____
_____

*Exercise 11.3 Types of Trauma*

*Type of Trauma (Circle One)*

Blunt     Sharp     Projectile     Other:_____

Justification: _____
_____
_____

*Exercise 11.4 Timing of Bone Injury*

*Timing of Injury (Circle One)*

Antemortem          Perimortem          Postmortem

**Justification:** _____

_____

_____

**Comments:** _____

_____

_____

**Exercise Worksheets 11.1 Through 11.4: Trauma Analysis (Copy 2)**

Name: _____   Date: _____

Case/Accession number: _____

*Exercise 11.1*

Description: _____

_____

_____

_____

_____

*Exercise 11.2*

Direction of force (circle one):

Tension                   Compression                Torsion

Bending                   Shearing                   Other: _____

Justification: _____

_____

_____

Speed of force (circle one):        Dynamic        Static

Justification: _____

_____

_____

Focus of force (circle one):        Narrow        Wide

Justification: _____

_____

_____

*Exercise 11.3*

*Type of Trauma (Circle One)*

Blunt        Sharp        Projectile        Other: _____

Justification: _____

_____

_____

*Exercise 11.4*

*Timing of Injury (Circle One)*

Antemortem          Perimortem          Postmortem

**Justification:** _____

_____

_____

**Comments:** _____

_____

_____

# 12 Projectile Trauma

Projectiles have distinctive wounding characteristics that make it unlikely that they will be mistaken for other types of trauma. Usually, bullets impact bone with so much force that they easily penetrate bone surfaces, causing the readily recognizable circular or oval entrance wounds. If they have enough energy, they will exit the bone, often leaving an irregular opening with jagged edges. Also, fracture lines are usually associated with both entrance and exit wounds. Because of these factors, forensic anthropologists can sometimes provide information on the type of firearm (e.g., handgun, rifle, or shotgun), characteristics of projectile (e.g., jacketed or hollow point), placement of the weapon in relation to the victim, and sequence of wounds (if multiple). You should be aware of these possibilities when analyzing this type of trauma, and when doing this lab.

## Learning Objectives

During this lab, you will learn the basic characteristics of projectile wounds: beveling, shape, size, and fracture lines. Once you are able to recognize these, you will learn about the nature of the wound, and the weapon that caused it.

## Expected Outcomes

By the end of this lab session, you should be able to:

* Recognize a bullet wound in the skeleton.
* Differentiate between entrance and exit wounds.
* Tell the direction of fire from the alignment of the entrance and exit wounds.
* Differentiate between simple gunshot wounds (more indicative of a handgun) and catastrophic wounds (more indicative of a rifle).

## Minimum Materials

Picture of human bone or structure (e.g., skull) with projectile trauma, preferably multiple views

## Optional Materials

Human bone or structure (e.g., skull) with projectile trauma (plastic or real)

## Exercise 12.1: Analysis of Projectile Wounds

Before proceeding, review the section Basics of Ammunition and Firearms in Chapter 12 of the textbook. Pay careful attention to how size is measured (i.e., caliber, gauge, or number), how bullets are constructed (including profile and jacketing), and how velocity affects the wounding power. In addition, review the section Basics of Bullet Travel.

Now, view the lab skeleton for any defects that resemble projectile wounds; this would include round or oval holes with or without fracture lines, massive fragmentation of bone (including the skull), or jagged openings in the brain-case. Once a hole is identified, check for wound beveling. If you are analyzing a skull, is the hole on the outside of the braincase smaller than the hole on the inside (internal beveling) or larger (external beveling)? Use Figures 12.2 and 12.3 of the textbook to familiarize yourself with these concepts. Now view the shape of the hole. Is it round (as in Figure 12.2 of the textbook), oval (as in Figure 12.5a), keyhole (Figure 12.7), or irregular (as in Figure 12.5b)? Next, measure the diameter of the circular or oval wound (if present). Using sliding calipers with opposing tips, measure

*Table 12.1* Relationship Between Caliber and Minimum Wound Size in the Human Skull

| Caliber of Bullet | Sample Size | Average Size of Wounds | Range of Wound Sizes | |
|---|---|---|---|---|
| | | | Minimum | Maximum |
| .22 | 37 | 0.27 | 0.22 | 0.45 |
| .25 | 5 | 0.26 | 0.24 | 0.30 |
| .32 | 6 | 0.34 | 0.26 | 0.43 |
| .38 | 25 | 0.43 | 0.34 | 0.69 |

From data in Ross AH (1996) Caliber estimation from cranial entrance defect measurements, Reprinted, with permission, from the *Journal of Forensic Sciences*, Vol. 41, Issue 4, copyright ASTM International, 100 Barr Harbor Drive, West Conshohocken, PA 19428. Her wound measurements converted to caliber.

the smallest and largest distances across the hole. Finally, trace the fracture lines, if present. Do they originate from a central location as in Figures 12.5a and 12.8, or do they surround a central area as in Figure 12.9? If a long bone is being analyzed, are butterfly fracture lines present (see Figure 12.6 of the textbook). Also, look to see if fracture lines end in another line or at a suture. Make a sketch of the bone(s) and wound(s) in the space provided at the end of the worksheet.

Now document the findings of your analysis on Exercise Worksheet 12.1. Start by describing the wound; be sure to include placement within the bone or structure (e.g., skull), and where the injury appears on the bone (i.e., proximal, middle or distal, medial or lateral, anterior or posterior). In addition, document the presence of beveling, and describe the relative shape of the wound and note the presence of fracture lines. For multiple wounds, give each a designation (e.g., A, B, C) to give your analysis more specificity (e.g., the sequence of wounds was B C A). Next, enter the size(s) as previously measured of any entrance wound(s), especially for injuries that have regular and well-defined margins (e.g., circular or oval entry wounds).

Now, if you are analyzing a skull, use Table 12.1 in this manual to estimate the caliber of the weapon that caused the bullet wound. Although this table has actual calibers listed, it is safer to use less specific descriptors: "small" for .22 and .25 caliber weapons, "medium" for .25 and .32 weapons, and "large" for .38 calibers or larger. In the area provided, justify your estimation of the caliber. Remember, do this only with circular or near circular bullet wounds; in cases where caliber cannot be estimated, simply state that on the worksheet.

Next, estimate the structure of the bullet by examining the exit wound, if any. Is it small and relatively round, or is it jagged and amorphous in outline? Is the bone relatively intact at the exit site, or is there extensive shattering and fracture lines? In the case of small and nearly circular exit wounds, jacketing of the bullet is indicated (although not certain); when the exit wound is accompanied by shattering of the surrounding bone, a soft-tipped bullet is indicated.

Now, try to determine the velocity of the bullet by observing the following features. Is there an exit wound (indicating high velocity)? Are there radiating or concentric fractures at the entrance wound? For wounds with extensive fracturing at the exit or entrance wounds, high velocity (and therefore, rifles or magnum handguns) is indicated; for injuries that do not exhibit an exit wound, low velocity (and therefore, handguns) is indicated. Write your estimate in the space provided on Exercise Worksheet 12.1 as well as your reasoning for this estimate. Next, use the shape and alignments of wounds to determine the placement of the weapon in relation to the victim. Is the entrance (or exit) wound round (indicating the bullet struck at a right angle), or is it oval (indicating an angular impact)? If there is an exit wound, pass a probe (e.g., wire or thin piece of plastic) through it and its opposing entry wound as in Figure 12.11 of the textbook. Write your findings in the direction of fire section of the worksheet.

Finally, attempt to determine the sequence of wounds if the lab skeleton has multiple injuries. First, locate the various bullet holes and identify those that are entrance wounds, using the information on beveling described earlier. Next, distinguish radiating from concentric fracture lines, and follow the radiating fractures out from their origin to their terminus. Find the wound that has fracture lines that do not end in another fracture line; this is the first wound in the sequence. Continue this process for all entrance wounds. Write your findings in the sequence section of the worksheet. Finish your analysis by writing any extra information that you feel is relevant in comments space of Exercise Worksheet 12.1 (e.g., self-inflicted, shooter possibly above victim).

## NOTE TO INSTRUCTORS

See the note in Chapter 11.

**Exercise Worksheet 12.1: Analysis of Projectile Wounds (Copy 1)**

Name: _____   Date: _____

Case/Accession number: _____

Description: _____

_____

_____

_____

_____

Entrance Wound(s)

A   Size: _____ by _____   Est. caliber:   Small   Medium   Large
          (length)              (width)

B   Size: _____ by _____   Est. caliber:   Small   Medium   Large
          (length)              (width)

C   Size: _____ by _____   Est. caliber:   Small   Medium   Large
          (length)              (width)

*Analysis*
**Estimation of caliber:**     Small     Medium     Large

Description: _____

_____

_____

Bullet construction: _____

_____

_____

Bullet energy: _____

_____

_____

Direction of fire: _____

_____

_____

Sequence (if multiple): _____

_____

_____

**Comments:** _____

_____

_____

**Sketch:**

**Exercise Worksheet 12.1: Analysis of Projectile Wounds (Copy 2)**

Name: _____ Date: _____

Case/Accession number: _____

Description: _____
_____
_____
_____
_____

Entrance Wound(s)

A    Size: _____ by _____    Est. caliber:    Small    Medium    Large
            (length)          (width)

B    Size: _____ by _____    Est. caliber:    Small    Medium    Large
            (length)          (width)

C    Size: _____ by _____    Est. caliber:    Small    Medium    Large
            (length)          (width)

*Analysis*
**Estimation of caliber:**    Small    Medium    Large

Description: _____
_____
_____

Bullet construction: _____
_____
_____

Bullet energy: _____
_____
_____

Direction of fire: _____
_____
_____

Sequence (if multiple): _____
_____
_____

**Comments:** _____

_____

_____

**Sketch:**

# 13 Blunt Trauma

Blunt trauma results when a force impacts a bone over a relatively wide area, causing discontinuities and fracture lines. Although clubs and other hand-wielded implements come first to mind when considering this type of injury, any hard surface such as the ground in a fall or a dashboard in an automobile accident can cause these types of injuries as well. The variety of instruments and surfaces that can produce this type of trauma is so great that specific aspects of the causative instrument may not be possible in many analyses. Therefore, be cognizant of the limits of the data available for your analysis when doing this lab.

## Learning Objectives

During this lab, you will learn the basic characteristics of blunt trauma to the human skeleton. Specifically, you will learn how blunt instruments affect bone when they are applied with dynamic or static force. Especially treated are the cranial vault and face, as these areas are often targets of such trauma, particularly in homicides.

## Expected Outcomes

By the end of this lab, you should be able to:

- Recognize blunt trauma on the skeleton.
- Estimate the size and shape of the causative instrument (if the injury lends itself to this type of analysis).
- Estimate the direction of travel (either of the instrument or of the body) at impact.
- Determine the number and sequence of injuries in cases of multiple injuries.

## Minimum Materials

Picture of human bone or structure (e.g., skull) with blunt trauma, preferably multiple views

## Optional Materials

Any human bone or structure (e.g., skull) with blunt trauma (plastic or real)
Human cranium with trauma to the braincase (plastic or real)
Human cranium with trauma to the face (plastic or real)

## Exercise 13.1: Analyzing Blunt Trauma to the Skull

Before attempting this analysis, review the basic aspects of bone trauma in Chapter 11 of the textbook. Also, review the section Characteristics of Instruments in Chapter 13 of the textbook that describes the aspects of instruments causing blunt trauma: size, shape, and weight. In addition, acquaint yourself with the natural buttresses of the skull. Those of the face, illustrated in Figure 13.1 of this manual, are malar eminences, nasofrontal processes, and alveolar ridges. Those of the braincase, illustrated in Figure 13.2, are midoccipital, posterior temporal, anterior temporal, and midfrontal. Finally, review the effects of trauma to the skull as illustrated in Figure 13.3 of this manual.

Now, using the lab skull or pictures, determine if there are fractures to the face or cranium. For trauma to the face, see if it fits into one of the LeFort fractures described in the textbook and illustrated in Figure 13.4 of this manual.

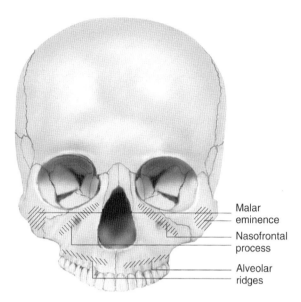

*Figure 13.1* Buttresses of the face.

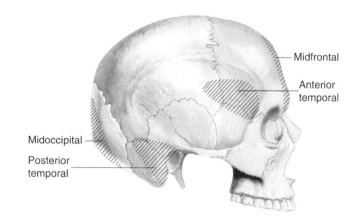

*Figure 13.2* Buttresses of the cranial vault.

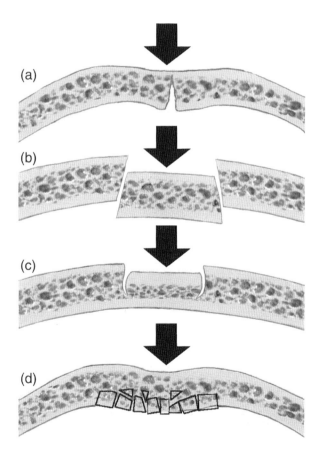

*Figure 13.3* Fractures characteristic of blunt trauma to the skull: (**a**) inbending at the impact site with concomitant fracture on the inner table; (**b**) formation of a plug in brittle bone; (**c**) crushing of the diploe; (**d**) crushing of the inner table.

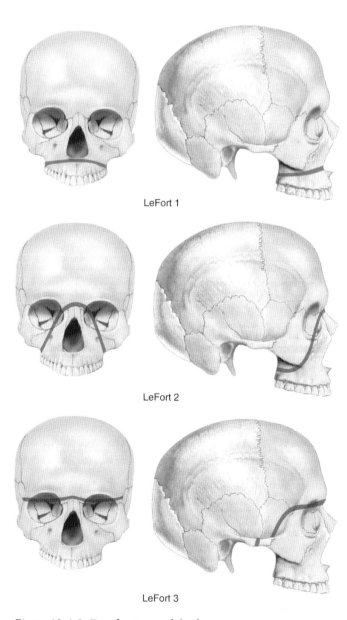

LeFort 1

LeFort 2

LeFort 3

*Figure 13.4* LeFort fractures of the face.

Notice the effect of the natural buttresses on the path of the fracture lines; the lines usually pass between these structures rather than through them (only very rarely will fracture lines pass through structures).

If the lab skull shows trauma to the braincase, determine if there is a complete fracture or infraction. In the case of an infraction, attempt to determine which of the categories shown in Figure 13.3 of this manual best illustrates the wound. If there are fracture lines, notice how they flow (in most cases) around the natural buttresses. In addition, try to determine the point of impact by noticing a central point (or points) from which the lines radiate.

Now, using Exercise Worksheet 13.1, perform a step-by-step analysis of the wound(s) you just studied. First, describe the trauma as precisely as you can. Note the bones affected (including side, if appropriate), the location of the injury within the bone, as well as the surface affected. Also note the amount of displacement (complete or incomplete), number of displacements (simple and comminuted), and the presence, as well as types, of fracture lines (radiating or concentric). Finally, for multiple wounds (as with projectile wounds), give each injury a designation (e.g., A, B, C) to give your analysis more specificity as you continue your work (e.g., the sequence of wounds was B→C→A). Also consider the direction of the causative force: tension, compression, torsion, bending, and shearing. Finally, estimate the size of the instrument causing the trauma, if possible. If there are distinct boundaries to the wound on the lab skull, measure the wound's length and width (if applicable) and depth (if an infraction).

If the injury is to the face, begin your analysis of the wound(s) by attempting to identify the LeFort fracture number. Remember, there can be multiple types to the facial area. Next, if the braincase is involved, describe the cross-sectional outline (e.g., circular, oblong, or angular) and axial configuration (straight, curved, or angular) of the wound. If a definite shape can be seen, try to imagine the causative instrument (e.g., crowbar with bent end, hammer, baseball bat). Enter your estimates in the shape area of Exercise Worksheet 13.1. Next, estimate the direction the instrument was traveling when it impacted the bone(s) by noting the side of the bone affected (e.g., superior, inferior, medial, lateral, right, left). Describe your estimates on the worksheet. Now try to estimate the amount of energy of the causative instrument. Are the injuries infractions (indicating low energy) or fractures (indicating high energy)? (As noted in the textbook, this is the result of both speed and weight of the causative instrument). Now, estimate the number of blows causing blunt trauma (if multiple injuries are present) by counting points of impact; these are areas from which fracture lines radiate, and can be surrounded by hoop fractures. Finally, determine the sequence of blows by using the same method as that for projectiles (see Chapter 12). Conclude your analysis by entering any more information concerning the blunt trauma in the comments area of the worksheet. If any of the information derived from your analysis can be used to determine that the injury(s) was self-inflicted, dispensed by another person, or was caused by the body impacting a hard surface, state it in this area.

## Exercises 13.2 A and 13.2 B: Analyzing Blunt Trauma to the Postcranial Bones

Analysis of trauma to postcranial bones follows the pattern given for skulls except that, instead of trying to identify LeFort fractures, the type of infraction or complete fracture is identified (if possible). Among infractions, Galloway (1999) recognizes seven types: bow, intraosseous, buckling, toddler's, vertical, green stick, and depressed. All of these, except the intraosseous type, are illustrated in Figure 13.5 of this manual. Among complete fractures, six are recognized: transverse, oblique, spiral, comminuted, butterfly, and segmented (Galloway, 1999); these are illustrated in Figure 13.6 of this manual. Two fractures are common enough to warrant special names: parry (Figure 13.7a of this manual) and Colles's (see Figure 13.7b of this manual). For any fractures to the postcranium, simply perform the steps given for the skull. First, determine if you are dealing with an infraction or a complete fracture. If an infraction, you will want to use Exercise Worksheet 13.2 A; if complete, use Exercise Worksheet 13.2 B. Now, describe the wound in detail, including the placement of the injuries on the skeleton in general and the bone in particular; enter this information in the space provided on the appropriate worksheet. Then, measure the boundaries of the trauma, and place the dimensions in the space provided. During this process, be open to the possibility that what you are observing is one of the special types described in the section *Basics of Bone Trauma* in Chapter 11 of the textbook: pathological, stress, or fatigue.

Analysis involves following the succession of elements already described. First, determine the type of fracture or infraction (if possible). Next, estimate shape, then direction of travel on impact, energy of impact, and sequence of traumatic events. Conclude your analysis by entering any additional information that you were able to glean during your analysis in the comments area of the worksheet.

## NOTE TO INSTRUCTORS

See note in Chapter 11.

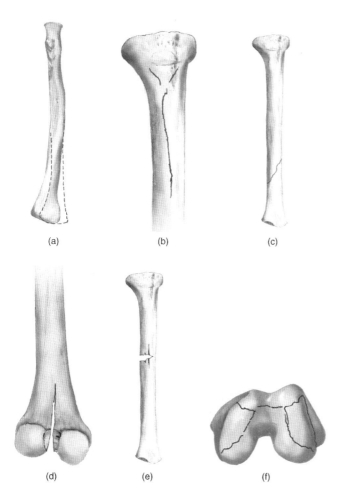

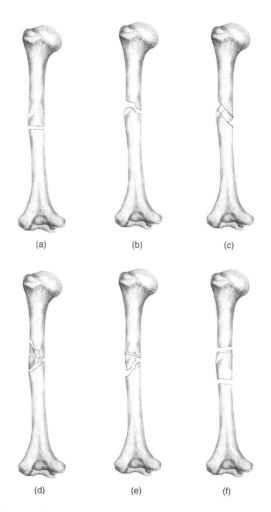

*Figure 13.5* Common infractions of the human skeleton: (a) bending fracture of the radius; (b) torus fracture of the proximal tibia; (c) toddler's fracture of the tibia; (d) vertical fracture of the distal femur; (e) green stick fracture of the tibia; (f) depressed fracture of the distal femur. After Figure 2-3 of Galloway (1999).

*Figure 13.6* Common complete fractures of the human skeleton (illustrated on the humerus): (a) transverse; (b) oblique; (c) spiral; (d) comminuted; (e) butterfly; (f) segmented. After Figure 2–4 of Galloway (1999).

*Figure 13.7* Fractures with special names: (a) parry fracture to the ulna; (b) Colles's fracture to the radius.

**Exercise Worksheet 13.1: Analyzing Blunt Trauma to the Skull**

Name: _____   Date: _____

Case/Accession number: _____

Description: _____

_____

_____

_____

_____

Size: _____ by _____ by _____
　　　　　(length)　　　　　　　(width)　　　　　　(depth)

*Analysis*

LeFort type (if to face; circle all that apply):　　　1　　　　2　　　　3

Shape: _____

_____

_____

Direction: _____

_____

_____

Energy: _____

_____

_____

Sequence: _____

_____

_____

Comments: _____

_____

_____

_____

_____

**Exercise Worksheet 13.2 A: Analyzing Blunt Trauma to the Postcranial Bones (Infractions)**

Name: _____ Date: _____

Case/Accession number: _____

Description: _____
_____
_____
_____
_____

Size: _____ by _____ by _____
    (length)      (width)      (depth)

*Analysis*

Type (circle all that apply):

Bow      Buckling      Toddler's      Vertical      Green stick      Depressed

Shape: _____
_____
_____

Direction: _____
_____
_____

Energy: _____
_____
_____

Sequence: _____
_____
_____

Comments: _____
_____
_____
_____
_____

**Exercise Worksheet 13.2 B: Analyzing Blunt Trauma to the Postcranial Bones (Complete Fractures)**

Name: _____ Date: _____

Case/Accession number: _____

Description: _____

_____

_____

_____

_____

Size: _____ by _____ by _____
    (length)      (width)     (depth)

*Analysis*

| Type (circle all that apply): | Transverse | Oblique | Spiral | |
|---|---|---|---|---|
| Comminuted | Butterfly | Segmented | Colles's | Parry |

Shape: _____

_____

_____

Direction: _____

_____

_____

Energy: _____

_____

_____

Sequence: _____

_____

_____

Comments: _____

_____

_____

_____

_____

# 14 Sharp and Miscellaneous Trauma

Along with projectile and blunt trauma, forensic anthropologists may encounter wounds caused by sharp instruments, as well as the fracturing of the hyoid bone from strangulation. Although more subtle, these two types of trauma can give important clues as to cause and manner of death. To analyze sharp trauma, all bones of the skeleton must be scrutinized for the characteristics of this type of injury. For strangulation, usually only the hyoid shows evidence of this cause of death; but other characteristics of this bone (e.g., age of the person at death) make fracture analysis difficult. Thus, perhaps more than any other lab, you must be especially vigilant when examining bone for these types of trauma.

## Learning Objectives

During this lab, you will learn the basics of sharp trauma to the human skeleton. Also, you will learn how to analyze this trauma for the basic characteristics of the causative instrument, direction of the sharp force, and number of traumatic events. In addition, you will learn to analyze the hyoid bone for evidence of death by strangulation (i.e., ligature, hanging, and manual strangulation).

## Expected Outcomes

By the end of this lab, you should be able to:

- Recognize the three types of sharp trauma to the skeleton: punctures, incisions, and clefts/notches.
- Make estimates about the causative instrument, the direction it impacted the body, and the number of traumatic events.
- Recognize those aspects of hyoid fracture that indicate strangulation.

## Minimum Materials

Picture of bone or structure (e.g., skull) with sharp force trauma, preferably with multiple views

## Optional Materials

Any bone with evidence of sharp trauma (plastic or real)
Entire skeleton, with some bones exhibiting sharp trauma (plastic or real)
Hyoid bones (fractured and whole)

## Exercise 14.1: Analyzing Sharp Trauma

Before attempting to analyze sharp trauma, familiarize yourself with the three different types: punctures, incisions, and clefts/notches (see Figure 14.1 in this manual) as well as the concepts of wastage and striations in the section Sharp Trauma in Chapter 14 in the textbook). Now, analyze the sharp trauma on the lab skeleton; that is, note any injuries that are V-shaped in cross section. Is the defect a puncture, an incision, or a cleft/notch? Use the characteristics in Table 14.1 in the textbook to help you determine this. Is the width narrow or wide? Is the depth shallow, medium, or deep? Is the length the same as the width? Use a handheld lens to see any striations in the defect. Are they vertical or

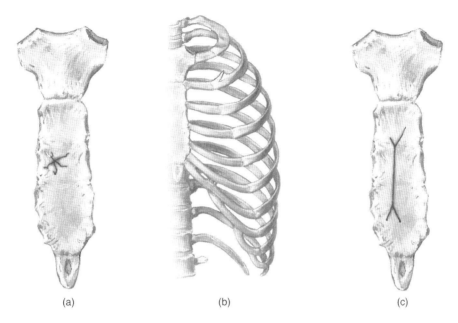

*Figure 14.1* Three basic types of sharp trauma: (**a**) puncture; (**b**) incision; (**c**) cleft.

horizontal? Are there fracture lines? Hinge fractures? Wastage? If the trauma is linear as in an incision, is the right arm the same or different from the left arm? Are striations (if present) coarse or fine? Finally, as with projectile trauma, give each wound (if multiple) a designation (e.g., A, B, C) to give your analysis more specificity (e.g., the sequence of wounds was B→C→A).

Now, use the table in Exercise Worksheet 14.1 as a decision matrix and circle each feature that is seen in the injury. Count the number of circles in each column and enter the totals on the bottom line of the table. Now, describe the wound in the area provided. In addition to the normal documenting of the location of each injury on the bone as well as the side and the location within the bone, include information on any associated fracture lines and segments of peeled bone. Finally, note the length, width, and depth of the wound, and place that information in the space provided.

Now, commence your analysis by estimating the instrument characteristics, such as type and size. Punctures are indicative of a stabbing instrument such as a knife, ice pick, or other such device. Knives can also cause incisions on bone. Finally, clefts and notches are indicative of chopping instruments such as axes, meat cleavers, and other such devices. After making your best estimate as to the type of instrument, add any information you may be able to glean on blade characteristics, such as length, width, surface contour (serrated or smooth), and sharpness.

Next, estimate the direction from which the force was applied to the bone(s); use the information from the textbook to help you in this endeavor. Did the instrument enter from the front, side, or rear? Was it applied in a downward, upward, or straight manner? Enter your estimates in the space provided on the worksheet. Finally, count the number of traumatic events, and estimate the sequence if multiple. How many points of impact are there? Are some of these paired (i.e., opposite each other on the front and back of the skeleton), or in line with each other as in Figure 14.8 in the textbook? Are there fracture lines? If so, use the method outlined in Chapter 12 of the textbook to determine this characteristic. Finish your analysis by noting any additional information on the traumatic event(s) you may have in the comments area of the worksheet (e.g., self-inflicted).

## Exercise 14.2: Analyzing Strangulation

Before attempting this analysis, review the section on Strangulation in Chapter 14 in the textbook for information on the three forms of this type of trauma (hanging, ligature, and manual strangulation) and the osteological implications of this cause of death on the hyoid bone. Now, view this bone on the lab skeleton. Is the proximal end of either of the cornua jagged (indicating a fracture), or smooth (indicating nonfusion)? Is the area where they attach to the body jagged or smooth? Enter the age at death of the lab skeleton in the space provided on the worksheet, and using this information, determine how likely it is that the hyoid was fused at the time of death (see Table 14.3 in the textbook). Now describe the hyoid and its concomitant fractures (if any). Also, comment on the likelihood that the hyoid is fractured (as opposed to unfused), and the probability that any fracturing is due to homicide (ligature or manual strangulation) or suicide (hanging). Document all of these findings on Exercise Worksheet 14.2.

## NOTE TO INSTRUCTORS

See note in Chapter 11.

**Exercise Worksheet 14.1: Analyzing Sharp Trauma (Copy 1)**

Name: _____   Date: _____

Case/Accession number: _____

| Characteristic | Punctures | Incisions | Clefts |
|---|---|---|---|
| Cross section | V-shaped | V-shaped | V-shaped |
| Width | Narrow or wide | Narrow or wide | Wide |
| Depth | Shallow or medium | Shallow or deep | Medium or deep |
| Length | Same as width | Short or long | Short or long |
| Striations | Vertical | Horizontal | Vertical |
| Fracture lines | Present | Absent | Present |
| Hinge fracture | Present | Absent | Present |
| Wastage | Minimal | Minimal | Significant |
| Arm Length | N/A | Left/Right/Same | N/A |
| Striation Granularity | N/A | Fine/Coarse | N/A |
| Total | _____ | _____ | _____ |

Partly taken from Reichs KJ (1998). Postmortem dismemberment: Recovery, analysis and interpretation. In KJ Reichs, editor. *Forensic Osteology Advances in the Identification of Human Remains*, 2nd edition. Courtesy of Charles C Thomas Publisher, Ltd., Springfield, Illinois.

Description: _____

_____

_____

_____

Size: _____ by _____ by _____
         (length)          (width)          (depth)

## Analysis

Circle type:        Puncture        Incision        Cleft/Notch

Justification: _____

_____

_____

Instrument characteristics: _____

_____

_____

Direction of force: _____

_____

_____

Number and sequence: _____

_____

_____

Comments: _____

_____

_____

_____

_____

## Exercise Worksheet 14.1: Analyzing of Sharp Trauma (Copy 2)

Name: _____ Date: _____

Case/Accession number: _____

| Characteristic | Punctures | Incisions | Clefts |
|---|---|---|---|
| Cross section | V-shaped | V-shaped | V-shaped |
| Width | Narrow or wide | Narrow or wide | Wide |
| Depth | Shallow or medium | Shallow or deep | Medium or deep |
| Length | Same as width | Short or long | Short or long |
| Striations | Vertical | Horizontal | Vertical |
| Fracture lines | Present | Absent | Present |
| Hinge fracture | Present | Absent | Present |
| Wastage | Minimal | Minimal | Significant |
| Total | _____ | _____ | _____ |

Partly taken from Reichs KJ (1998). Postmortem dismemberment: Recovery, analysis and interpretation. In KJ Reichs, editor. *Forensic Osteology Advances in the Identification of Human Remains*, 2nd edition. Courtesy of Charles C Thomas Publisher, Ltd., Springfield, Illinois.

Description: _____

_____

_____

_____

_____

Size: _____ by _____ by _____
     (length)      (width)     (depth)

## Analysis

Circle type:          Puncture          Incision          Cleft/Notch

Justification: _____

_____

_____

Instrument characteristics: _____

_____

_____

Direction of force: _____

_____

_____

Number and sequence: _____

_____

_____

Comments: _____

_____

_____

_____

_____

**Exercise Worksheet 14.2: Analyzing Strangulation (Copy 1)**

Name: _____   Date: _____

Case/Accession number: _____

Age at death: _____

Description: _____

_____

_____

_____

_____

Comments: _____

_____

_____

_____

_____

**Exercise Worksheet 14.2: Analyzing Strangulation (Copy 2)**

Name: _____ Date: _____

Case/Accession number: _____

Age at death: _____

Description: _____

_____

_____

_____

_____

Comments: _____

_____

_____

_____

_____

# 15 Antemortem Skeletal Conditions

As pointed out in the textbook, almost all skeletons exhibit some sort of deviation from the norms developed through the study of human osteology. These deviations can be divided into three basic types: pathological conditions (changes in shape and size of bones), anomalies (accessory ossicles, nonfusions, accessory foramen, and miscellaneous), and markers of occupational stress. For you to be able to recognize each of these three types, you will have to have a good idea of what is "normal" for the human skeleton.

## Learning Objectives

During this lab, you will learn the basics of pathological conditions, anomalies, and indicators of occupational stress. Specifically, you will learn how to recognize the three basic pathological changes to bone: bone loss, bone gain, and bone deformation. In addition, you will learn the basic nature of anomalies: accessory bones, nonfusions, accessory foramen, and miscellaneous changes. Finally, you will learn the four types of occupational stress markers: modifications to areas of insertion, osteophytosis, discrete markers, and stress fractures.

## Expected Outcomes

By the end of this lab, you should be able to:

- Recognize the three antemortem conditions that can occur in the human skeleton.
- Recognize lytic, deformative, and proliferative pathological conditions.
- Recognize accessory bones, nonfusions, accessory foramen, and miscellaneous anomalies.
- Distinguish modifications to areas of insertion, osteophytosis, discrete markers, and stress fractures from each other, and interpret what they tell you about the life of the person before death.

## Minimum Materials

Picture(s) of any human bone with a pathological condition, anomaly, or indications of occupational stress

## Optional Materials

Human skeleton with pathological conditions, anomalies, or indications of occupational stress (plastic or real)

### Exercise 15.1: Analyzing Pathological Conditions

Before analyzing the laboratory skeleton for pathological conditions, familiarize yourself with the three types: lytic, proliferative, and deformative (see the section Pathological Conditions in Chapter 15 of the textbook). Now, view the skeleton for lytic bone changes. Are there perforations of the occipital bone of the skull (Figure 15.5a of the textbook)? Are there holes in bones where they do not belong that may indicate localized bone death (Figure 15.1 of this manual; Figures 15.1a and 15.5b of the textbook)? Pay particular attention to the superior and inferior surfaces of the vertebral bodies (the so-called Schmorl's node pictured in Figure 15.6 of the textbook) and the alveolar area (abscess; Figure 15.7 of the textbook).

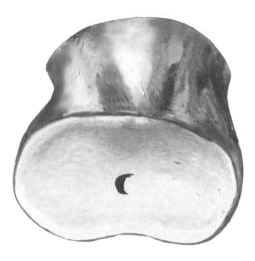

*Figure 15.1* Lytic lesion of the proximal articular surface of the first phalange of the big toe.

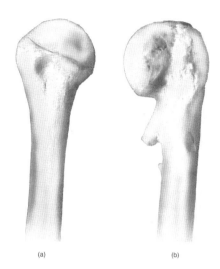

(a)                              (b)

*Figure 15.2* Osteoproliferative lesion of the proximal humerus: **(a)** normal humerus; **(b)** callus with osteophytic extensions.

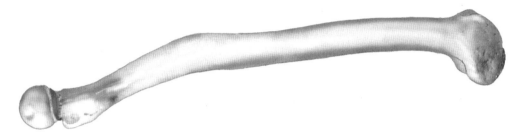

*Figure 15.3* Deformative lesion of the femur apparently caused by the imperfect healing of a fracture.

Next, view the skeleton for proliferative lesions. Are there spurs of bone growing out of the anterior part of the vertebral bodies (Figure 15.2 of the textbook)? Look for similar outgrowths around the articular areas of all bones. Do any of the shafts of long bones (especially the tibia) have striations on the otherwise smooth cortical surface (Figure 15.8)? Are there any calluses on long bones indicating healing or healed antemortem breaks (Figures 15.9 in the textbook, and 15.2 of this manual)? How about the skull; are there any button osteomas (Figure 15.10 in the textbook)?

Finally, view the skeleton for any deformitive lesions. Are any of the bones bent in an unusual manner (Figures 15.3 of this manual and 15.9a of the textbook)? Are any of the vertebral bodies "wedged," causing kyphosis or scoliosis (Figure 15.11 of the textbook)? Now, using Exercise Worksheet 15.1, document all of the pathological conditions you observed on the skeleton. Be sure to indicate the bone affected, the area on the bone, the type of lesion, and any other information that you can glean. Be careful about diagnosing the possible cause of the lesion; this requires more experience than can be gained from a class of this nature.

### Exercise 15.2: Analyzing Skeletal Anomalies

In this section of the lab, you will look for some of the many anomalies that appear in the human skeleton; familiarize yourself with their description in the section Skeletal Anomalies in Chapter 15 of the textbook. There are four different types of anomalous conditions: accessory ossicles, nonfusion anomalies, accessory foramen, and miscellaneous anomalies. To ascertain if the laboratory skeleton manifests any of these, familiarize yourself with the bones of the cranium and postcranium (Chapter 2 of the textbook). Now, view the lab skull for any accessory bones, nonfusion

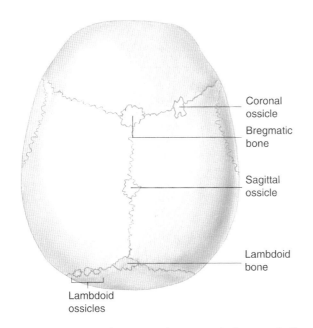

*Figure 15.4* Sites of accessory bones on the human skull (superior view).

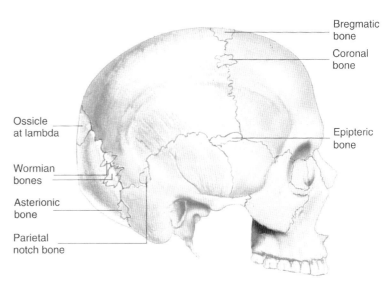

*Figure 15.5* Sites of accessory bones on the human skull (lateral view).

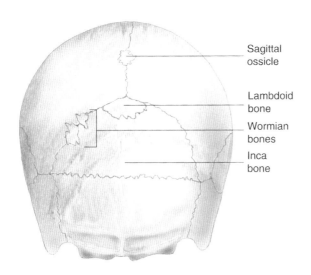

*Figure 15.6* Sites of accessory bones on the human skull (posterior view).

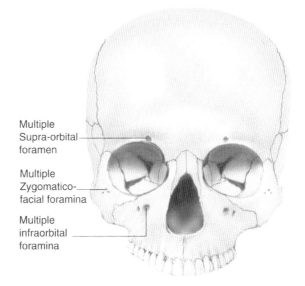

*Figure 15.7* Sites of accessory foramen on the human skull (anterior view).

anomalies, accessory foramen, and miscellaneous abnormalities. Use Figures 15.4, 15.5, and 15.6 of this manual and Figures 15.17 and 15.18a of the textbook as a guide for accessory bones. Also, see Figure 15.18b of the textbook for an example of a nonfusion anomaly, and Figure 15.7 of this manual for accessory foramen. Are there any extra bones in the suture lines, such as the coronal, sagittal, lambdoid, and squamosal sutures? Are any of the bones divided in half (e.g., occipital, frontal)? Are there any extra foramen on the face or skull base? Finally, are there any trephinations indicating antemortem medical treatment?

Now, view the rest of the skeleton. Are there any unfused parts of the vertebrae (particularly the neural arches to the bodies) as in Figure 15.19a of the textbook? Are the neural arches of the sacrum fully fused to each other, or are they open (spina bifida) as in Figure 15.19b of the textbook? Do any of the bones appear in two parts without evidence of fracture (e.g., nonfused scapula as in Figure 15.8 or bipartite patella as in Figure 15.9 of this manual)? Are any of

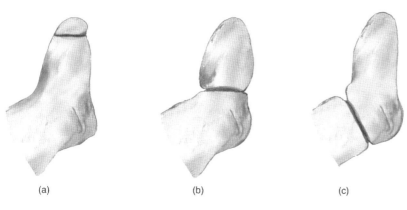

(a)                          (b)                          (c)

*Figure 15.8* Common sites of nonfusion of the acromion of the scapula: (a) tip;
(b) segment just distal to angle; (c) segment just proximal to angle.

*Figure 15.9* Common nonfusions of the patella.

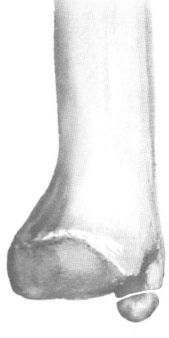

*Figure 15.10* Nonfusion of the styloid process of the
ulna (persistent ulna styloid ossicle).

*Figure 15.11* Nonfusion of the posterior process of
the talus (os trigonium).

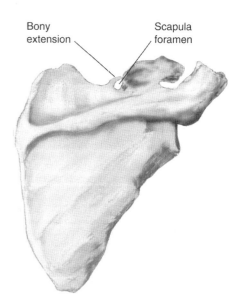

Bony
extension

Scapula
foramen

*Figure 15.12* Foramen at the site of the scapular notch.

the processes on bones (e.g., styloid process of the ulna) not fused with their concomitant bone (Figures 15.10 and
15.11 of this manual)? (Be sure to examine the joining surfaces for smooth cortical bone.) Do any of the bones have
foramen where they do not belong, such as the sternum (Figure 15.20 of the textbook), humerus (Figure 15.27a of
the textbook), or scapula (Figure 15.12 of this manual)? Use Exercise Worksheet 15.2 to document those seen in the
lab skeleton.

## Exercise 15.3: Analyzing Occupational Stress Markers

View the lab skeleton for examples of occupational stress markers. As described in the section Occupational Stress Markers in Chapter 15 of the textbook, there are four types: modifications to areas of insertion, osteophytosis, discrete markers, and (stress) fractures. Using Table 15.1 of this manual, view the bones listed in the left-hand column for the enlarged areas of muscle attachment (hypertrophies) given in the middle column of the table. Do any of these bones have the types of enlarged areas given in the table? Do the same with Tables 15.2, 15.3, and 15.4 of this manual for osteophytes, discrete markers, and stress fractures, respectively. Document each finding on Exercise Worksheet 15.3 and include a hypothesized cause from the right-hand column of the tables. Be very careful in your wordings, as these causes are not the only possible origins of the conditions that you may find.

*Table 15.1* Lesions of Insertion Areas From Occupations/Activities of Industrialized Countries

| Bone or Structure | Muscle/Structure | Occupation/Activity |
| --- | --- | --- |
| Mandible | Lateral pterygoid (sharp tubercles on condyles) | Clarinet, or other woodwind, playing |
| Humerus | Pectoralis major and deltoid Medial epicondyle | Kayaking, Golfing |
| Radius | Tuberosity | Masons and bakers |
| Ulna | Supinator crest | Fruit picking, iron workers |
| | Triceps brachii exostoses | Baseball playing |
| Hands | Palmer insertions of proximal phalanges | Grasping writing tool, holding paddle or oar |
| Femur | Gluteal tuberosity, linea aspera | Football players, horseback riders |
| Calcaneous | Achilles tendon, adductor hallicus | Joggers |
| | Plantar fascia (bony spurs) | Policemen, floorwalkers |

Reduced from Table 1 of Wilczak and Kennedy (1998).

*Table 15.2* Osteophytosis From Occupations/Activities of Industrialized Countries

| Bone or Structure | Affected Area | Occupation/Activity |
| --- | --- | --- |
| Vertebrae | Bodies of C4, C5, C6, and C7 | Fruit pickers |
| Shoulder | Glenoid cavity with wrist affected | Pneumatic drill |
| Elbow | Primary capitulum and radial head | Kayaking |
| | Lateral epicondyle of humerus | Tugging on extended arm (e.g., dog walking) |
| Knee | Lateral and medial surfaces of femur, tibia, and patella | Martial arts, walking in deep snow |
| Foot | 1st and 5th metatarsal | Walking over rough terrain |
| | 1st metatarsal | Golfing |

Reduced from Table 2 of Wilczak and Kennedy (1998).

*Table 15.3* Discrete Markers of Occupations/Activities of Industrialized Countries

| Bone or Structure | Affected Area | Occupation/Activity |
| --- | --- | --- |
| Ear | Auditory exostoses | Divers |
| Vertebrae | Kyphosis of spine | Tailors, weavers, shoemakers, factory workers |
| | Scoliosis of spine | Carrying burdens on one shoulder |
| | Scmorl's node | Heavy labor |
| Chest | Fusion between manubrium and body with concavity of sternum and ossification of 1st rib | Shoemaker |
| | Flattened ribs with flattened spines in T5 through L5 | Wearing a back brace |
| Clavicle | Robusticity at acromial end | Milkmen |
| | Robusticity at sternal end | Hand sewing |
| Glenoid | Superior facet with slight humeral head flattening and deltoid hypertrophy | Fruit pickers |
| Acromion | Bipartite | Fruit pickers |
| Ulna | Hypertrophy of proximal half | Rodeo cowboys |
| Ankle | Facets on the anterior of the distal tibia, and superior surface of the neck of the talus | Squatting |
| Ischium | Craggy tuberosity | Sitting for long periods |
| Foot | Extension of metatarsal–phalangeal articulation | Canoeing and other activities with kneeling |
| Incisors | Dented edges | Holding things in teeth (e.g., nails) |
| Premolars | Ellipsoid aperture | Pipe smoking |

Reduced from Table 3 of Wilczak and Kennedy (1998).

*Table 15.4* Fractures Associated With Occupations/Activities of Industrialized Countries

| Bone | Condition | Occupation/Activity |
| --- | --- | --- |
| Vertebrae (middle and lower) | Separation of neural arch from vertebral body | Heavy lifting |
| | Anterior wedging | Travel in vehicles with poor shock absorption, parachuting |
| Radius | Bilateral stress fracture | Bakers, masons |
| Ulna | Chipping at notch with exostoses on medial surface | Baseball pitchers |
| Thumb | Transverse fracture | Rodeo or mechanical bull-riding |
| Calcaneous | Exostoses and fractures | Impact of heel on ground (e.g., dismounting after riding) |

Reduced from Table 4 of Wilczak and Kennedy (1998).

### NOTE TO INSTRUCTORS

Some of the conditions that are the subject of this lab are available as casts from the sources described in the Sources of Materials section at the beginning of this manual. However, it may be difficult to find specimens of the anomalies and markers of occupational stress. Although many skeletons show at least one of these, they may not be depicted in the budget-priced plastic casts (which do not have the detail of real bone), or even the more expensive casts.

**Exercise Worksheet 15.1: Analyzing Pathological Conditions**

Name: _____ Date: _____

Case/Accession number: _____

Lytic conditions: _____

_____

_____

_____

_____

Proliferative conditions: _____

_____

_____

_____

_____

Deformative conditions: _____

_____

_____

_____

_____

Comments: _____

_____

_____

_____

_____

**Exercise Worksheet 15.2: Analyzing Skeletal Anomalies**

Name: _____   Date: _____

Case/Accession number: _____

Accessory bones: _____

_____

_____

_____

_____

Nonfusion anomalies: _____

_____

_____

_____

_____

Accessory foramen: _____

_____

_____

_____

_____

Miscellaneous anomalies: _____

_____

_____

_____

_____

Comments: _____

_____

_____

_____

_____

**Exercise Worksheet 15.3: Analyzing Occupational Stress Markers**

Name: _____ Date: _____

Case/Accession number: _____

Age of Person: _____

Modifications to areas of insertion: _____
_____
_____
_____
_____

Osteophytosis: _____
_____
_____
_____
_____

Discrete markers: _____
_____
_____
_____
_____

Stress fractures: _____
_____
_____
_____
_____

Comments: _____
_____
_____
_____
_____

# 16 Postmortem Changes to Bone

Chapter 16 in the textbook provides information on the types of damage that can occur to bone after death. Although caused by an almost infinite number of forces, only the most common of these postmortem changes will be the subject of this lab. The first part deals with damage caused during dismemberments, while the second part deals with the host of natural forces that can affect bone.

## Learning Objectives

During this lab, you will become acquainted with the characteristics of postmortem bone damage. This damage can result from one, or more, of six sources: humans, nonhuman animals, fire, weather, soil, and water.

## Expected Outcomes

By the end of this lab, you should be able to:

- Analyze bone damage due to dismemberments, including estimating saw width, number of teeth, blade shape, and source of energy.
- Recognize differences between bone damage due to carnivores and damage caused by rodents.
- Recognize the four different types of carnivore bone damage: punctures, pits, scoring, and furrows.
- Estimate the amount of shrinkage from the color of burned bone.
- Recognize damage caused by weathering, burial, and water transport.

## Minimum Materials

Bones with saw damage (do not have to be human)

## Optional Materials

Bones with carnivore or rodent damage
Bones burned to different colors
Bone with weather, burial, or water transport damage

## Exercise 16.1: Analyzing Saw Marks

Before commencing the analysis of saw marks, review the section Basics of Saws and Saw Damage in Chapter 16 of the textbook. Now, start with a thorough description of the cuts seen in the lab bones. How many cuts, false starts, or superficial false start scratches can be seen? On what bone are they located, and within the bone, on which part can they be seen (anterior or posterior, medial or lateral, proximal or distal)? Now, using a sliding caliper with opposing tips, measure the widths of the kerfs (see Figure 16.1a of this manual) from sectioned bones with breakaway spurs or incomplete cuts. Using this measurement, and considering that tooth set is usually not more than 1.5 times the blade width, what does the measurement of the kerf tell you about the width of the saw blade?

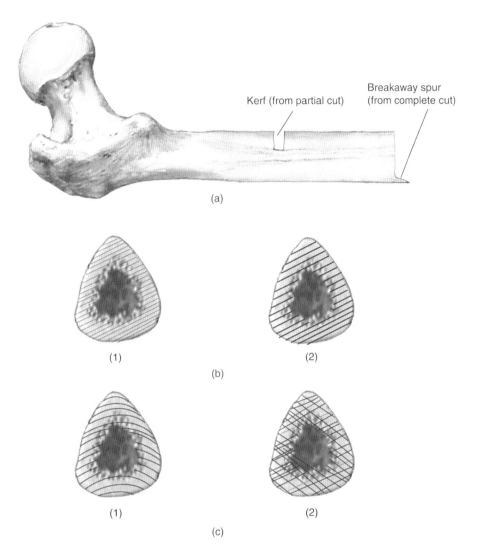

*Figure 16.1* Diagram of characteristics of cut marks caused during dismemberment: (**a**) femur showing kerf due to incomplete cut and breakaway spur, both of which could be measured for saw blade width; (**b**) femoral cross section showing striations due to a (**1**) fine-bladed saw, and (**2**) coarse-bladed saw; (**c**) configuration of striations due to (**1**) a fixed-radius (e.g., circular) saw, and (**2**) a straight-bladed saw.

Next, try to determine the direction of the saw progress. On what side of a bone are the superficial false starts or incomplete cuts? On what surface are the breakaway spurs (see Figure 16.1a)? False starts on the anterior surface of a bone, or a breakaway spur on its posterior side, indicate that the saw operator started at the front of the bone (probably with the victim lying on his or her back) and cut in a downward direction. View either side of the cut. Is there exit chipping on one side but not another? What does that tell you about the direction of the push stroke if a hand saw was used?

Now try to determine whether the type of saw used had coarse or fine teeth. Are there rough gouges along the sides of the cut (see Figure 16.1b [2] of this manual), or are there thin striations on the kerf walls (see Figure 16.1b [1])? Next, examine the shape of the striae on the kerf walls. Do they have a fixed radius (i.e., form concentric arched lines; see Figure 16.1c [1] of this manual), indicating a circular blade? Or are the striae relatively straight (these may, or may not, be parallel to each other; see Figure 16.1c [2]) indicating a rigid straight blade, or do they curve up toward the direction of the cut, indicating a nonrigid straight blade? Is the kerf floor W-shaped (indicating a crosscut saw) or flat (indicating a rip saw)? Now, observe the kerf walls. Are they uneven both in flatness and saw progress with coarse, straight striae? Or are the kerf walls smooth, almost polished, with fixed-radius striae? Once you have completed your analysis, fill out Exercise Worksheet 16.1. Be as complete as possible in your descriptions and measurements. Also, be careful of your conclusions; do not go beyond what the data allow.

## Exercise 16.2: Analyzing Other Postmortem Damage

In this section, you will analyze the type of damage caused by carnivores and rodents, fires, weathering, burial, and water transport.

### Animal Scavenging

Although animals have three major effects on human skeletons (i.e., bone scattering, breakage through trampling, and removal of bony elements by chewing), this lab will concentrate on the result of carnivore and rodent chewing. Before commencing, familiarize yourself with the effects of these animals by reading the section Animal Scavenging in the textbook. Now, try to determine if the damage seen in the lab specimen is caused by a carnivore or a rodent. Is the damage in the form of straight grooves with relatively flat floors (indicating rodents), or are the floors sharp (indicating carnivores)? Do the grooves come in opposing pairs that meet to form a tip (again indicative of a rodent)? Can the damage be described as punctures (i.e., areas of bone that have collapsed under the pressure of a carnivore tooth), pits (areas of bone collapse that do not penetrate through the cortical bone), scoring (scratches across the cortical surface), or furrows (scoring that is deeper and found at the ends of bone)? Are any of these types of damage accompanied by fracture lines, splintering, or depressed fractures? Now, fill in the Animal Scavenging section of Exercise Worksheet 16.2. First, describe the damage that you see, and then respond to each of the subheadings on the worksheet. Make your answers as complete as possible.

### Fire Damage

Familiarize yourself with the section Fire Damage in the textbook before commencing this part of your analysis. As described, the main use of information on fire damage is its effect on bone dimensions (especially length) due to shrinkage. Observe the lab bone and use the information in Table 16.1 of the textbook to determine the approximate temperature of burning and the amount of shrinkage. Also, is there warping (e.g., bending, twisting), or does the cortex exhibit cracks that have a checkerboard or crescent shape? Are there breaks that are longitudinal, or are there transverse or oblique ring fractures? Now, complete the Fire Damage section in Exercise Worksheet 16.2.

### Weathering

Before commencing this part of the lab, read the section Weathering in Chapter 16 of the textbook. Now, analyze the lab bone for the effects of weathering, mainly sunlight. Does the damage appear as a mosaic or set of parallel-sided cracks over the bone's surface? Has the topmost layer begun to separate and flake off, exposing the underlying cortex? Is the cortical bone beginning to flake off in concentric layers, causing the bone eventually to disintegrate? Are there longitudinal cracks, similar to those seen in fire and burial? Is there warping (bending, twisting), similar to that seen in burning, due to uneven drying? Now, complete the Weathering section in Exercise Worksheet 16.2.

### Burial Damage

Before analyzing any damage due to burial, read the appropriate section in the textbook. Now, observe the lab bone for cracking and warping similar to that seen in fire and weathering. Are there longitudinal fractures in the long bones? Do broken bones exhibit breaks with relatively flat (nonjagged) surfaces? Does the cortical bone exhibit erosion (loss of outer layer, pitting)? Now, fill in the Burial Damage section in Exercise Worksheet 16.2. Make your answers as complete as possible.

### Water Transport Damage

Before starting this section, read Water Transport Damage in Chapter 16 of the textbook. Now, try to distinguish any damage to the lab skull (information on water damage to other skeletal elements is unknown as of this writing). Are the thin bones of the face (e.g., lacrymals, ethmoid) and cranial vault (e.g., greater wing of the sphenoid) broken? Is there evidence of abrasion (e.g., pitting, scratching, gouging) of various projecting anatomical features of the skull? Is the mandible present, or lost postmortem during transport? Does the skull exhibit staining from algae, hardening of silt in various orifices forming a crust on the surface, or deposition of aquatic insect egg casings? Now, complete the Water Transport Damage section in Exercise Worksheet 16.2.

## *Miscellaneous*

As mentioned at the end of Chapter 16 in the textbook, there are a host of other forces that can cause postmortem damage. Using the last section of Exercise Worksheet 16.2, describe the damage that you see as best as possible. Then, try to identify the source of the damage by circling the appropriate response to the possible cause query. Last, make any comments that you think are appropriate in the space provided.

## *NOTE TO INSTRUCTORS*

The materials for this lab can be emulated by using nonhuman bone. A trip to a pet store that sells bones for dogs to chew, or to a butcher shop, will yield bones that you can modify with saws, fire, water, and burial. (As you probably noticed, I did this for the photos in Chapter 16 of the textbook exhibiting saw marks as I did not want to sacrifice human bone for these figures.) Although this is not the same as human bones exhibiting postmortem damage, the effects are similar enough that students will have a good experience analyzing what you have created.

## Exercise Worksheet 16.1: Analyzing Saw Marks

Name: _____   Date: _____

Case/Accession number: _____

Description: _____

_____

_____

_____

_____

### Direction of Saw Progress (Circle Appropriate Response)

Anterior to posterior          Posterior to anterior

Medial to lateral          Lateral to medial

Justification: _____

_____

_____

### Direction of Stroke (Circle Appropriate Response)

Anterior to posterior          Posterior to anterior

Medial to lateral          Lateral to medial

Justification: _____

_____

_____

Number of teeth (circle correct response):      Coarse          Fine

Justification: _____

_____

_____

Blade width = _____ ÷ 1.5 = _____
                (kerf width)

**Blade type/kerf floor:**          Crosscut/W-shaped          Rip/Flat

**Blade shape (circle one):**          Fixed radius          Nonfixed (straight)

**Justification:** _____

_____

_____

**Saw power:** _____

_____

_____

**Comments:** _____

_____

_____

## Exercise Worksheet 16.2: Analyzing Other Postmortem Damage

Name: _____ Date: _____

Case/Accession number: _____

### Animal Scavenging

Description: _____

_____

_____

_____

_____

Types of marks (circle all that apply):

    Punctures          Pits          Scoring          Furrows

    Splintering          Depressed fractures          Fracture lines

Type of animal (circle all that apply):

    Carnivore          Rodent

Comments: _____

_____

_____

_____

_____

### Fire Damage

Description: _____

_____

_____

_____

_____

**Color (Circle One)**

   White, yellow, brown, gray, black

   White, gray, blue

   White

**Approximate shrinkage (circle one):**

   0%–2%                    1%–3%                    5%–25% (9.5% average)

**Type of fractures (circle all that apply):**

   Checkerboard             Crescent

   Longitudinal             Ring

Comments: _____

_____

_____

_____

## Weathering

Description: _____

_____

_____

_____

_____

**Types of damage (circle all that apply):**

   Mosaic                   Flaking                  Concentric flaking

   Longitudinal cracks      Bending                  Twisting

Comments: _____

_____

_____

_____

_____

## Burial Damage

Description: _____

_____

_____

_____

_____

Type of fractures (circle all that apply):

Checkerboard            Crescent

Longitudinal            Ring

Comments: _____

_____

_____

_____

## Water Transport Damage

Description: _____

_____

_____

_____

Breakage (circle all that apply):

Lacrymals              Ethmoid              Maxilla

Frontal (eye orbits)   Sphenoid

Palatines              Other:_____

Other (circle all that apply):

Algae staining             Silt in orifices

Aquatic insect egg casings Other:_____

Comments: _____

_____

_____

_____

## Miscellaneous Damage

Description: _____

_____

_____

_____

_____

**Possible Cause (Circle All That Apply)**

Root damage            Excavation damage

Deposition of minerals     Cortical erosion

Other: _____

Comments: _____

_____

_____

_____

# 17 Additional Aspects of Individualization

Although previous chapters have presented numerous methods for analyzing the skeleton, there are several other methods that can determine further characteristics of an individual. The first, facial reproduction, involves developing a face from the skull, while the second, determining body weight, is based on the analysis of the skeleton. These methods of individualization are the second to last techniques used in the forensic analysis of the human skeleton.

## Learning Objectives

During this lab, you will learn the steps for constructing a reproduction of a face on a skull using clay and prostheses (i.e., glass eyes, wigs). In addition, you will make the observations and measurements needed to assign living body weight to people from their skeletal remains.

## Expected Outcomes

By the end of this lab, you should be able to:

- Make a reproduction of the face of a person from his or her skull.
- Estimate the living body weight from skeletal (and other) remains.

## Minimum Materials

Human skull (plastic or real)
Dowels ($\frac{1}{8}$" in diameter) or pencil erasers
Glue
Clay or Plastocene (approximately 2 pounds)

## Optional Materials

Sculpting tools
Scale (for weighing bones)
Height/weight charts from National Institutes of Health
Real and complete human skeleton

## Exercise 17.1: Facial Approximation

Before starting facial reproduction, ascertain the demographic characteristics (i.e., ancestral group, sex, age) and any other information concerning the decedent (e.g., dress or pants size, shirt size, etc.). Now, using the information in Table 17.1 in this manual, cut the dowels or erasers to the lengths specified for each location on the skull. Using Figure 17.1 of this manual as a guide, glue these spacers onto their respective locations (see Figure 17.2a of the textbook). Next, insert artificial eyes in the ocular orbits using clay to get the proper orientation (see Figure 17.2b of the textbook); dark eyes can be used in Blacks and Asians, while light eyes may be appropriate with Whites. As noted in the textbook, the protrusion (anterior position) of the glob within the eye orbit has received considerable attention over the years. As of this writing, the best estimate is that this structure should protrude approximately 16 millimeters from the deepest point on the lateral orbital margin. The medial–lateral and superior–inferior placement of the eye glob should be such that the pupil is slightly superior and lateral to the center of the eye orbit. (More specifically, the pupil is inferior 46.6% of the total distance between the superior and inferior orbital margins, and lateral 42.6% of the distance between the lateral and medial orbital margins.) Also, the corners of the eyelids (canthi) should be in line with the malar tubercle (a small bulge medially on the inferiolateral border of the eye) on the lateral side and the lacrimal fossa (a furrow on the lacrimal bone) on the medial side. Finally, the distance between the canthi should be 75% of the distance between the medial and lateral orbital margins, and the distance between the orbital margins and the canthi should be approximately the same on the medial and lateral sides.

Now, on a flat surface, roll out slabs of clay or Plastocene approximately as thick as the dowels/erasers are long and approximately ½" wide. Use these to connect the areas between the spacers as in Figure 17.3a of the textbook.

*Table 17.1* Adult Standards of Facial Tissue Thicknesses for All Groups[1]

| Site Number | Location–Definition | Mean (mm) | Standard Deviation (mm) |
|---|---|---|---|
| **Median Points** | | | |
| g | Glabella—See Chapter 2 | 5.5 | 1.0 |
| n | Nasion—See Chapter 2 | 6.5 | 1.5 |
| rhi | Rhinion—Most inferior point on the internasal suture | 3.0 | 1.0 |
| sn | Subnasale—See Chapter 2 | 12.513.0 | 3.0 |
| ls | Labrale superius—See prosthion in Chapter 2 | 11.5 | 3.0 |
| li | Labrale inferius—Most anterior point between the medial lower incisors | 13.0 | 2.53.0 |
| mls | Mentolabial sulcus—deepest point on the mandible above the mental eminence | 11.0 | 2.0 |
| gn | Gnathion—See Chapter 2 | 87.5 | 3.0 |
| **Lateral Points** | | | |
| mso | Mid-supraorbital—Point on the superorbital rim at the midsagittal plane of the orbit | 6.5 | 1.52.0 |
| mio | Mid-infraorbital—Point on the infraorbital rim at the midsagittal plane of the orbit | 7.0 | 3.0 |
| zy | Zygion—Most lateral point on the zygomatic arch | 67.0 | 1.02.5 |
| acp | Alare curvature point—Point ca. 3 mm lateral to the nasal aperture | 9.5 | 2.5 |
| mr | Mid-ramus—Point on the center of the ascending ramus | 18.5 | 4.5 |
| sM² | Supra-M²—Point on the maxillary alveolar ridge superior to the second molar | 25.0 | 5.5 |
| iM₂ | Infra-M₂—Point on the mandibular alveolar ridge inferior to the second molar | 18.5 | 4.5 |
| go | Gonion—See Chapter 2 | 11.5 | 6.0 |
| mmb | Mid-mandibular border—The mid-point on the inferior margin of the mandible | 11.5 | 4.5 |

[1]Abridged from Table 3 of Stephan (2014).

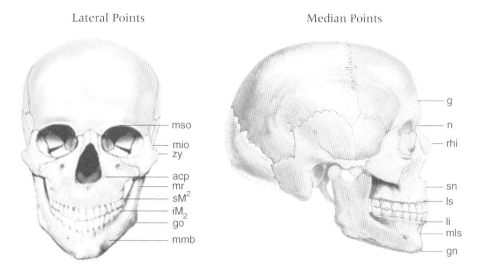

*Figure 17.1* Location of points used in facial reproduction.

Next, use the formulae below to determine the width of the nose in life.

Living width for Whites = Opening width + 12.2                                      (1)

Living width for Blacks = Opening width × 1.63                                    (2)

If desired, erect a scaffold on the nose to account for the soft tissues lost during decomposition; make it appropriate for the ancestral group: for Whites, a high structure is used, while in Blacks and other groups, it is flatter. Using Figure 17.2 in this manual, place the pronasale (line PH) such that it is approximately one-fifth of the way up a line connecting nasion and a point approximated by subnasale (line NaS). The maximum projection of pronasale (line PP in Figure 17.2 in this manual) anterior to a line connecting nasion and the most posterior point on the maxilla below the nasal aperture (line NaM in Figure 17.2 in this manual) is approximately 60.5% of that length in males (PP = 0.605 × NaM) and 56% in females (PP = 0.56 × NaM).

After formation of the nose, the mouth should be approached. Although several methods have been offered for determining the width of this structure, the easiest is to set the width of the mouth at 133% of distance between the lateral borders of the canines.

Now apply the last layer, simulating the skin, over the preceding clay (see Figure 17.3b of the textbook). If the person is of Asian ancestry, sculpt an epicanthic fold over the superior and lateral parts of the eyes. If there is information indicating that the person may be of Chinese ancestry, add fat pads under the eyes. In addition, if the ancestry is considered Black or Southeast Asian, apply thick, everted lips to the reproduction. Also, if the person is older, wrinkles around the eyes (more pronounced after 30), mouth, and forehead may be in order. Similarly, for persons over 50, the lateral edges of the eyelids should droop such that pupils of the eye are partially obscured. Next, add a wig to give realism to the reproduction (Figure 17.3b of the textbook), short hair for males, long hair for females. Again, use information on ancestral groups for this trait (i.e., straight black hair for Asians, wavy and light or dark color for Whites, dark and curled for Blacks). Finally, add facial hair to males (if there is evidence of this from the recovered remains), and add eyebrows for realism. Remember, the desired result is a reproduction that is average in appearance so that it can be recognized by a wide variety of people. (There is no exercise worksheet for this exercise.)

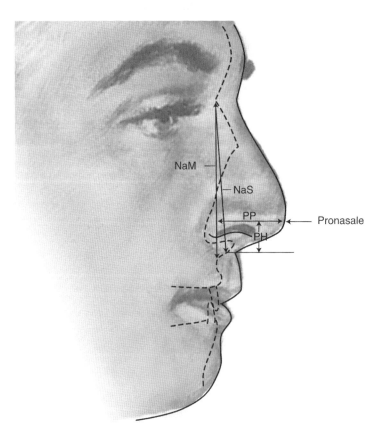

*Figure 17.2* Lines and measurements used to determine the placement of pronasale (the most forward point on the nose).

## Exercise 17.2: Estimating Body Weight

Attempt to determine the body weight of the individual represented by the skeleton by using the four factors of sex, muscle markings, height, and skeletal robusticity. Thus, first determine sex using the methods of Chapter 8, and stature using the methods described in Chapter 10. Next, consult a medical height/weight chart, such as that created by the Metropolitan Life Insurance Company (this can be found on various websites such as www.halls.md/ideal-weight/met.htm), to determine skeletal robusticity (called frame size) of the lab specimen. Once that has been determined (small, medium, large), find the weight of the person by matching sex, height, and robusticity against the appropriate chart. Finally, if clothing was found at the recovery scene, use information on its size to get an idea of body build (e.g., small dress sizes and narrow waist trousers would indicate thin, and therefore light, people).

*Table 17.2* Determination of Living Weight of Males From Skeletal Weight

| Regression Equations | Standard Error |
|---|---|
| **Whites** | |
| Living weight = 0.024 (dry skeletal weight) + 50.593 | 20.1 |
| Living weight = 0.233 (dry femur weight) + 57.385 | 22.2 |
| **Blacks** | |
| Living weight = 0.013 (dry skeletal weight) + 85.406 | 13.7 |
| Living weight = 0.163 (dry femur weight) + 76.962 | 13.3 |

Taken from Baker and Newman (1957); bone weight is in grams, body weight in pounds.

Now, weigh all of the bones of the skeleton and use the regression formulae in Table 17.2 in this manual to determine living weight. Finally, document all of these findings on Exercise Worksheet 17.2 and make an estimate of final weight. It may be most useful to describe the decedent's build as "slight," "medium," or "heavy," or more simply, "lean" versus "overweight." Finally, justify your estimate in the comments area of the worksheet.

## *NOTE TO INSTRUCTORS*

This may be one of the easiest labs because the materials for facial reproduction are relatively inexpensive. Plastic skulls are best for this task as the thin bones of the eye orbits and nose of a real skull may be injured by the application of clay. Only the exercise on body weight may be costly as the balances used to weigh bone can be expensive.

**Exercise Worksheet 17.2: Estimating Body Weight (Copy 1)**

Name: _____ Date: _____

Case/Accession number: _____

Sex: _____

Height: _____

Muscle markings (circle one):     slight     medium     large

Robusticity (circle one):     slight     medium     large

Weight range (from ht/wt charts): _____ to _____

Calculated weight: _____ × _____ + _____ = _____
                        (bone weight)   (coefficient)    (intercept)       (weight)

Most likely weight: _____

Comments: _____

_____

_____

_____

_____

_____

**Exercise Worksheet 17.2: Estimating Body Weight (Copy 2)**

Name: _____  Date:_____

Case/Accession number: _____

Sex:_____

Height:_____

**Muscle markings (circle one):**        slight        medium        large

**Robusticity (circle one):**        slight        medium        large

**Weight range (from ht/wt charts):** _____ to _____

**Calculated weight:** _____ × _____ + _____ = _____
                          (bone weight)      (coefficient)       (intercept)        (weight)

**Most likely weight:**_____

Comments: _____

_____

_____

_____

_____

_____

# 18 Obtaining an Identification

As described in the textbook, there are two types of identifications of human remains: positive and probable. Both involve the comparison of antemortem information with the postmortem osteological elements to determine if a positive, or highly probable, match exists between these two sources. Positive identifications are based on comparing radiographs or implanted surgical/dental devices, while probable identifications combine a number of concordant points to make it highly probable that the remains are from the person represented by the antemortem data.

Since most of the techniques described in Chapter 18 of the textbook are too complex for a lab of this nature, only two exercises are presented here. In the first, you will compare antemortem and postmortem radiographs of osteological structures such as sinuses or ends of long limb bone to determine if there is a match between the two. In the second exercise, you will perform a point-by-point comparison of dental structures to determine if the antemortem records match the human remains.

## Learning Objectives

The exercises in this chapter will assist you in developing the creative thinking skills necessary to work toward positive or probable identification of complete and incomplete human remains. This includes describing the similarities and differences between antemortem and postmortem radiographs of osteological structures (e.g., frontal sinus) used for this purpose. Also, you will compare photographs of people and skulls to experience the process for excluding a person or obtaining a probable identification.

## Expected Outcomes

Upon completion of the following exercises, you should be able to:

- Recognize various osteological structures observable in radiographs.
- Conduct a point-by-point comparison of osteological structures and measurements between antemortem and postmortem radiographs, report the points of agreement and disagreement, and conclude or exclude a positive identification.
- Do a point by point comparison of photographs of people and skulls to exclude a person or conclude a probable identification.

## Minimum Materials

Copies of pairs of antemortem and postmortem radiographs of any bone
Copies of pairs of antemortem and postmortem radiographs of frontal sinuses

## Optional Materials

Photographs/portraits of people and skulls (facial views)

## Exercise 18.1: Identification From Radiographs

In this exercise, you will use antemortem and postmortem skeletal radiographs to make a positive identification or exclusion. As stated in the textbook, the method for concluding a positive identification from a comparison of antemortem and postmortem radiographs requires complete agreement of all observable attributes. The analysis takes place by comparing, point by point, the osteological structures present, as well as defined measurements.

Look at the pairs of antemortem and postmortem radiographs that illustrate matching points of comparison provided for you. Carefully and critically observe each point of comparison and answer the following questions. Can you see the osteological structures indicated? If you are able to see them, do they appear to be identical? Do the borders of the bones in the radiographs have the same configuration? If the metaphyseal area is displayed, does the trabecular bone match between the two? Would you feel confident in concluding a positive identification? How many points of similarity do you think are necessary to conclude a positive identification? How many points of disagreement can exist and still have a positive identification? Should there be a minimum number of points of similarity required before a positive identification is made?

If you cannot see the identified structures, why do you think this is the case? Is it due to the quality of the radiograph or, perhaps, your inexperience in evaluating radiographs? Do you think practicing forensic anthropologists have the same problems observing the structures? Summarize the factors that can affect a forensic anthropologist's ability to accurately compare x-rays.

Now that you have gained some experience reading and comparing radiographs, look at a set of unlabeled antemortem and postmortem x-rays. Using Exercise Worksheet 18.1, identify and label points of agreement and disagreement. Pay particular attention to the borders of the bones and the configuration of the trabecular bone (if present). Enter your conclusion regarding identification, and explain your decision.

## Exercise 18.2: Identification From Photographic Superimposition

In this exercise, you will compare the photograph of a skull with that of a person in an attempt to determine if they represent the same individual. First, ensure the two images are the same size. In the past, the images could be made into slides and placed into different slide projectors, where the sizes could be made the same by moving a projector away from the screen to enlarge an image or away to make it smaller. If they are digital images, use appropriate software. Whatever method is used, superimpose the two images so that the most superior point on the skull (vertex) and inferior border of the mandible match these same features on the person's photo. The basic analysis involves searching for points of concordance between the bony landmarks of the skull with those parts of a portrait where there is little soft tissue to obscure these landmarks. Thus, the position of the eye orbits, nasal aperture, and ear openings and the spacing and configuration of the dentition are compared for agreement. In addition, the general size and shape of the skull, especially the length and width of the face and height of the forehead, also are compared.

Now complete Exercise Worksheet 18.2 by noting the points of concordance. Are the faces the same width? Does the pyriform aperture align with the nose? The eye with the eye orbits? Ears and external acoustic meatus? Circle the appropriate answer on each line. Now note, on the lines provided, any other points of concordance between the two images. When complete, circle whether you feel the two images are from the same person, and make any comments you feel are appropriate.

## *NOTE TO INSTRUCTORS*

For this lab, you will need to compile a set of antemortem and postmortem x-rays of various skeletal structures so that they can be arranged side by side. Most of the sets should have the points of comparison identified. The points of comparison of one or two of the sets should *not* be labeled; the student groups will be asked to identify some points of similarity or dissimilarity. The sets can consist of photocopies of those published in various books or copies of actual radiographs. You can contact your local coroner, medical examiner's office, or even hospitals for more. (As long as the case number and patient name is removed, they may let you make copies.) If you have access to actual radiographs, it is best if they are scanned into a computer. Working with scanned radiographs allows you to crop the image as necessary and to set up various comparisons—some that match and some that do not. Regardless of whether you have actual radiographs or photocopies of radiographs, you need to construct unlabeled (as to points of agreement/ disagreement) sets of antemortem and postmortem x-rays that match and that do not match. Students will be asked to compare the unlabeled x-rays and reach a conclusion regarding identification.

For the face/skull superimposition, it would be best if you can obtain photos of dead persons and their skulls. However, since this can be difficult, you can use the portraits of any person (dead or alive) and compare it with the facial view of any skull. Although you would know that the two could not be the same, the students would still be able to do a point-by-point comparison and exclude the person in the picture.

**Exercise Worksheet 18.1: Identification From Radiographs (Copy 1)**

Name: _____   Date: _____

Case/Accession number: _____

## Anthroposcopy

Points of concordance: _____

_____

_____

_____

Conclusion (circle one):          Same person          Different person

Comments: _____

_____

_____

_____

**Exercise Worksheet 18.1: Identification From Radiographs (Copy 2)**

Name: _____  Date: _____

Case/Accession number: _____

## Anthroposcopy

Points of concordance: _____

_____

_____

_____

Conclusion (circle one):      Same person          Different person

Comments: _____

_____

_____

_____

**Exercise Worksheet 18.2: Identification From Skull/Face Superimposition**

Name: _____   Date: _____

Case/Accession number: _____

## Points of Concordance

Facial Widths Same:               Yes      No

Nose Placement Same:              Yes      No

Eyes Align With Orbits:           Yes      No

Ears Align With Acoustic Meatus:  Yes      No

Other Concordances: _____

_____

_____

Conclusion (circle one):      Same person          Different person

Comments: _____

_____

_____

_____

# 19 Conclusion

The final chapter in the textbook presents four topics of significant interest to all forensic anthropologists: ethical responsibilities, preparation and content of the final report, courtroom testimony, and the future of forensic anthropology. Of these, this lab will concentrate on the final report and courtroom (expert witness) testimony. Some of the exercises presented here represent activities that should be done before the end of the term, and others that represent the culmination of all of your hard work throughout the course.

Galloway et al. (1990) provide an excellent summary of the legal and ethical responsibilities of forensic anthropologists. These range from those associated with the practice of forensic anthropology—the application of the theories, knowledge, and methods of human osteology and skeletal biology—to those related to achieving and maintaining the educational and experiential qualifications necessary to practice forensic anthropology. Also considered to be an ethical responsibility is the participation in the criminal justice system as an expert through consultation on casework and the communication of the evidence analyzed, methods used, and the results, conclusions, and interpretations both in a written report and, when necessary, as expert testimony in the courtroom.

## Learning Objectives

The projects outlined for this chapter are designed to provide you with a capstone experience that incorporates the knowledge you gained throughout the course. First, you use your prior labs to produce a summary report for a particular case. Then, you will design an oral presentation that effectively communicates to an audience the nature of the case, the methods applied during the analysis phase, a summary of the conclusions reached, and the evidentiary foundation (what you observed) for each of them. After your "testimony," you will need to clearly and effectively respond to questions from a group of your peers. Finally, you will judge the effectiveness of another's oral presentation.

## Expected Outcomes

Upon completion of this assignment, you should be able to:

* Complete a summary of all data forms related to a case analysis.
* Present a well-organized and effective oral presentation of the case analysis.
* Pose informed and knowledgeable questions for use in the cross-examination of a peer group.
* Develop clear, informed, and knowledgeable responses to the cross-examination of your group.
* Have an understanding of what contributes to effective questioning of experts, as well as effective expert testimony.

## Minimum Materials

Your labs for the semester to use as a forensic anthropology case

## Optional Materials

Videos or access to courtrooms, *Court TV*, or any other venue through which to observe expert testimony

## Exercise 19.1: Forensic Anthropology Report

The project presented here consists of three parts. The first part is a forensic anthropology case analysis. This requires that you have access to all of your labs for the semester. The second part is the composition of a final report summarizing the methods applied and conclusions reached during the analysis of the skeletal remains. The final component of this project is the oral presentation of your case and your testimony during a cross-examination by a group of your peers. You may choose to do one, two, or all three of the assignments depending on time constraints.

Review the section The Final Report in Chapter 19 in the textbook before beginning this assignment. Now, working in groups of two or three people, depending on the size of the class, conduct a complete forensic anthropological skeletal analysis using the exercise worksheets from the semester. Following the analysis, submit a final skeletal report on Exercise Worksheet 19.1. The final skeletal report will present and summarize the results of the application of all the bone identification and methodological techniques you have learned during this course. Following the completion of the osteological analysis of your assigned forensic case, you will communicate the results of your analysis in a report that will consist of an introduction to the case (including the circumstances of its discovery and recovery, when and who called you in as a consultant, and a summary of your results), a skeletal inventory, determination of minimum number of individuals represented, ancestry, sex attribution, age-at-death determination, stature estimation, any perimortem trauma that may relate to cause and/or manner of death, a description and interpretation of any pathologies and anomalies that may assist in a positive identification, and a bibliographic listing of all sources used during the analysis.

The final report should consist of all data sheets, including:

Summary of analysis
Skeletal inventory
Attribution of ancestry
Attribution of sex
Estimation of age at death
Calculation of stature
Skeletal trauma, pathologies, and anomalies

These data forms should be appended to a three- to five-page, typed summary report. This report should summarize the information from your data sheets; both your conclusions and how you arrived at them. For example, state the determined age and sex of the individual, as well as the criteria used to determine sex and the methods used to determine age. While writing your report, consider that your audience includes members of the medicolegal community (e.g., medical examiners, attorneys, law enforcement) and that it could become a document of the court so a typographic mistake could affect your legitimacy and success as a scientific expert.

Feel free to consult with your classmates regarding the application and results of the various techniques; this discussion goes on frequently between forensic consultants. The final report and conclusions, however, should be your own.

## Exercise 19.2: Expert Witness Testimony Evaluation

This assignment will be conducted in conjunction with the group forensic anthropological case presentations. Each case presentation will be 15 minutes in length, and will present a summary of the forensic case analyzed over the course of the semester. Your presentation will focus on the analytical techniques applied, conclusions reached, and interpretations of the conclusions reached. You are encouraged to highlight an interesting and unique aspect of your case (i.e., cause of death; challenging circumstances). Visuals of some sort (PowerPoint, overheads, slides, drawings) are required and will facilitate an understanding of your area of expertise by the "jury."

Following each case presentation, a cross-examination of the "consulting forensic anthropologist" will take place by a team of "attorneys." The course instructor will determine the team responsible for cross-examination of each forensic anthropology team. The cross-examination will focus on a limited aspect (or a couple of aspects) of the forensic case. Groups conducting the cross-examination must inform the professor of the focus of their questioning at least 5 days before the presentations in order to give the team some direction for preparation, and to avoid duplication of questions. Each member of the cross-examination team and each member of the forensic anthropology consulting team must ask and answer questions for this assignment.

Miscellaneous information:

> Each forensic anthropology consulting team must provide opposing counsel with a draft report no later than 7 days prior to the presentation and cross-examination.
> Each team of attorneys must inform the professor and the forensic anthropology consulting team of the focus of their cross-examination no later than 5 days before the cross-examination; topics go on a first-come, first-serve basis.
> A list of questions to be asked must be submitted to the professor on the day of the cross-examination, but before it begins.
> Each team will be graded on its presentation of the forensic case, its effectiveness in answering questions during cross-examination, and the quality of the questions asked during cross-examination.

As discussed in the section Courtroom Testimony in the textbook, forensic anthropologists are increasingly called to testify as expert witnesses. The ability of the experts to clearly explain what they did, how they did it, and why they came to the conclusions they did, in a manner that is understandable to a jury composed (typically) of nonscientists is very important. If forensic scientists cannot communicate in a manner that is understandable to the jury, its members may disregard what the expert is saying, or even misinterpret what is said.

Consider and discuss among your classmates how well the "experts" in this exercise communicate their results. Consider the impression they make—demeanor, clothing, vocabulary—and how this affects their effectiveness in explaining what they did, how they did it, and why they reached the conclusions they are presenting. Use Exercise Worksheet 19.2 to record your thoughts. Alternatively, you can do this in realistic settings such as in a local courtroom or on television (e.g., *Court TV*).

## *NOTE TO INSTRUCTORS*

This lab could easily take 2 weeks to complete. During the first week, you could have your students assemble the forms they completed during the term into a complete forensic analysis. They then could write the three- to five-page summary based on these forms. The following week would involve having some students provide "expert testimony" on their findings, with other students acting as prosecuting and defending attorneys as well as the jury (you could preside as judge). This mock courtroom is very instructive in that it shows how well students comprehend the material in the class, despite the parts they play. For example, the students who provide the testimony must be well versed in the methods of forensic anthropology; however, so must those playing the jury or they will not recognize errors of omission or errors of inclusion (testimony not supported by the facts).

**Exercise Worksheet 19.1: Forensic Anthropology Report**

### Summary of Analysis

Name: _____  Date: _____

Case number: _____

Condition: _____

_____

_____

Time since death: _____

Ancestry: _____

Sex: _____

Age at death: _____

Stature: _____

Trauma: _____

_____

_____

Unique characteristics: _____

_____

_____

**Exercise Worksheet 19.2: Expert Witness Testimony Evaluation**

Name: _____    Date: _____

Case/Accession number: _____

Name of expert witness: _____

Location of trial: _____

Area of expertise: _____

Witness for (circle one):            Prosecution            Defense

1.  How effective is the expert witness in explaining what he or she does and what his or her conclusions are?

    _____

    _____

    _____

    _____

    Why do you think this witness was effective? Why not?

    _____

    _____

    _____

    _____

2.  How did the experts respond to the questioning by the prosecution attorney(s)? Defense attorney(s)?

    _____

    _____

    _____

    _____

3.  What is your interpretation of the effectiveness the expert testimony had on the trial? Was the testimony significant to the case? Examine the information presented, in what demeanor, and its understandability.

    _____

    _____

    _____

    _____

If you said the testimony was significant, why?

_____

_____

_____

_____

If you said the testimony was not significant, why?

_____

_____

_____

_____

4.  What factors of expert witness testimony affect its contribution to a case?

_____

_____

_____

_____

# References

Adams BJ, Herrmann NP (2009) Estimation of living stature from selected anthropometric (soft tissue) measurements: Applications for forensic anthropology. *Journal of Forensic Sciences*, 54(4): 753–760.

Baker PT, Newman RW (1957) The use of bone weight for human identification. *American Journal of Physical Anthropology*, 15: 601–618.

Bass WM (1995) *Human Osteology: A Laboratory and Field Manual*, 4th edition. Columbia, MO: Missouri Archaeological Society.

Bass WM (1997) Outdoor decomposition rates in Tennessee. In: WD Haglund, MH Sorg, editors. *Forensic Taphonomy*, pp. 181–186. New York: CRC Press.

Bass WM (2005) *Human Osteology: A Laboratory and Field Manual*, 5th edition. Columbia, MO: Missouri Archaeological Society.

Brues AM (1977) *People and Races*. New York: Macmillan.

Buikstra JE, Ubelaker DH (1994) *Standards for Data Collection from Human Skeletal Remains*. Fayetteville, AR: Arkansas Archeological Survey Research Series #44.

Cornwall IW (1956) *Bones for the Archeologist*. New York: MacMillan.

France DL (1998) Observational and metric analysis of sex in the skeleton. In: KJ Reichs, editor. *Forensic Osteology Advances in the Identification of Human Remains*, 2nd edition, pp. 163–186. Springfield, IL: Charles C. Thomas, Publisher.

Galloway A (1999) *Broken Bones: Anthropological Analysis of Blunt Force Trauma*. Springfield, IL: Charles C. Thomas, Publisher.

Galloway A, Birkby WH, Jones AM, Henry TE, Parks BO (1989) Decay rates of human remains in an arid environment. *Journal of Forensic Sciences*, 34: 607–616.

Galloway A, Birkby WH, Kahana T, Fulginiti L (1990) Anthropology and the law: Legal responsibilities of forensic anthropologists. *Yearbook of Physical Anthropology*, 33: 39–57.

Gilbert BM (1973) *Mammalian Osteo-Archaeology: North America*. Columbia, MO: The Missouri Archaeological Society.

Gilbert BM, Marin LD, Savage HG (1981) *Avian Osteology*. Laramie, WY: B. Miles Gilbert, Publisher.

Giles E (1970) Discriminant function sexing of the human skeleton. In: TD Stewart, editor. *Personal Identification in Mass Disasters*, pp. 99–109. Washington, DC: National Museum of Natural History, Smithsonian Institution.

Giles E (1991) Corrections for age in estimating older adults' stature from long bones. *Journal of Forensic Sciences*, 36: 898–901.

Giles E, Elliot O (1962) Race identification from cranial measurements. *Journal of Forensic Sciences*, 7: 147–157.

Giles E, Elliot O (1963) Sex determination by discriminant function analysis of crania. *American Journal of Physical Anthropology*, 21: 53–68.

Gill GW, Gilbert BM (1990) Race identification from the midfacial skeleton: American blacks and whites. In: GW Gill, JS Rhine, editors. *Skeletal Attribution of Race*, pp. 47–53. Anthropological Papers #4. Albuquerque, NM: Maxwell Museum of Anthropology.

Gordon CC, Churchill T, Clauser CE, Bradtmiller B, McConville JT, Tebbetts I (1989) 1988 Anthropometric survey of U.S. Army personnel: Methods and summary statistics. Technical Report NATICK/TR-89/044. Natick, MA: U.S. Army Research, Development, and Engineering Center.

Haglund WD (1997) Dogs and coyotes: Postmortem involvement with human remains. In: WD Haglund, MH Sorg, editors. *Forensic Taphonomy*, pp. 367–382. New York: CRC Press.

Heaton V, Lagden A, Moffatt C, Simmons T (2010). Predicting the postmortem submersion interval for human remains recovered from UK waterways. *Journal of Forensic Sciences*, 55(2): 302–307.

Hefner JT (2009) Cranial nonmetric variation and estimating ancestry. *Journal of Forensic Sciences*, 54(5): 985–995.

Hefner JT, Pilloud MA, Black CJ, Anderson BE (2015) Morphoscopic trait expression in "Hispanic" populations. *Journal of Forensic Sciences*, 60(5): 1135–1139.

İşcan MY, Loth SR, Wright RK (1984) Age estimation from the rib by phase analysis: White males. *Journal of Forensic Sciences*, 29: 1094–1104.